Three Contributions to the Theory of Sex

Three Contributions to the Theory of Sex

BY SIGMUND FREUD

Translated from the German by A. A. Brill

INTRODUCTION BY HENDRIK M. RUITENBEEK

FOREWORDS BY JAMES J. PUTNAM AND A. A. BRILL

NEW YORK

E. P. DUTTON & CO., INC.

Published simultaneously in Canada by
Clarke, Irwin & Company Limited,
Toronto and Vancouver.

SBN 0-525-47105-7

INTRODUCTION

Three Contributions to the Theory of Sex "stands, there can be no doubt, besides his (Freud's) *Interpretation of Dreams* as his most momentous and original contribution to human knowledge."[1] This book is Freud's major statement on the nature and development of sexuality in the human being. Yet, although psychoanalysis has become part of the background of the average educated man, most lay readers still have only a superficial understanding of Freud's concepts about sexuality. Hence, reissuing these essays in convenient paperback form is particularly useful. Nor is renewed interest in these essays inappropriate for professional psychotherapists themselves, since so many of them, in the United States and Europe alike, have tended to minimize both sexuality and its role in the origins of neurosis.

It has been observed that the post-Darwinian world has invented two new religions: communism and psychoanalysis. If the first is distinguished by the enforcement apparatus of orthodoxy, the second may be characterized by the multiplication of heresies. Many of those "heresies," which are deviations from, or revisions of, Freudian theory, sprang from opposition to Freud's emphasis on the fundamental sexual basis for human behavior, both individual and social. When Jung, Adler, and Otto Rank—all notable among Freud's early disciples—came to differ with Freud and abandoned part of his theory, their differences were based on Freud's ideas about accepting the centrality of sex. Many other psychologists who have drawn inspiration from Freud have modified his theories drastically, again largely because they disagreed with Freud's excessive emphasis on the role of instinct, and particularly on the instinct of sex.

[1] P. 126, James Strachey (ed.), *The Standard Edition of the Complete Psychological Works of Sigmund Freud,* Vol. VII, London, Hogarth Press and The Institute of Psychoanalysis, 1953.

In these three essays, which constitute so important a part of Freud's work, he presents the core of his thesis that the neurotic person's experience is of such nature that he clings to the infantile aspects of his sexuality. Whereas the person who achieves a normal maturity passes through the phases of infantile sexuality and leaves most of these behind, the neurotic person finds it difficult to do so. He preserves infantile sex attitudes and behavior in many disguises, as it were, and often eventually reverts to some infantile form of sex expression. With this picture of human development in his mind, it was logical that Freud should focus his interest on sexual development in the child.

Most respectable people in Freud's time, however, regarded the child as a peculiarly pure creature. And no creature could be considered "pure" if it were tainted by sexuality. To be sure, the Christian infant might be redeemed from the world, the flesh, and the devil at his baptism, but by the end of the nineteenth century, many people regarded that pledge as a mere ceremonial gesture. If any being on earth were innocent, it was the infant in his cradle or the toddler at his mother's knee. To suggest that the infant drew in libidinous delight with his mother's milk, and to assert that the toddler expressed enjoyment, anger, and many other pleasurable emotions in his refusal to be housebroken was, as Ernest Jones comments, "a calumny on the innocence of the nursery."[2]

Stendhal, however, in the autobiography he calls the *Life of Henri Brulard* has given a vivid picture of himself as a young boy in his mother's arms, jealous of any other man who approached her, and most jealous of the man with clearest legal right to do so. I quote from the book:

> My mother, Madame Henriette Gagnon, was a charming woman, and I was in love with her. I hasten to add that I lost her when I was seven years old.
>
> In loving her at the age of perhaps six (1798), I had exactly the same character as when, in 1828, I loved Albertae de Rubempré with a mad passion. My way of starting on the quest for happiness had not changed at

[2] P. 286, Ernest Jones, *The Life and Work of Sigmund Freud*, Vol. II, New York, Basic Books, 1955.

> all in essentials, with this sole exception—that in which constitutes the physical side of love I was what Caesar would be, if he had come back to earth, with regard to the use of cannon and small arms. I should soon have learned, and it would have changed nothing essential in my tactics.
>
> I wanted to cover my mother with kisses, and for her to have no clothes on. She loved me passionately and often kissed me—I returned her kisses with such ardor that she was often obliged to go away. I abhorred my father when he came and interrupted our kisses. I always wanted to give them to her on her bosom. Be so good as to remember that I loved her, in childbed, when I was barely seven.[3]

But Stendhal was only beginning to be esteemed as a novelist when these three essays by Freud were first published in 1905, and the reader who was shocked by the theories of the relentlessly probing Viennese physician was equally disturbed by the French novelist.

Although Freud offered these theories to a public rather less officially inhibited than that of late Victorian England or the United States (which was shocked when President Theodore Roosevelt's daughter, Alice, was rumored to have smoked a cigarette), he was still addressing audiences, professional and lay alike, that had a deep-rooted fear of sexuality. For sex is the force in man which is hardest to control and therefore most in need of bridling.

Yes, in spite of all the changes in our *mores* which have occurred since the early 1900's, Western society (and America in particular) still has this basic fear of sex. Nowhere perhaps has Western society experienced more radical changes than in the United States; nowhere perhaps is sex a more marketable commodity, yet our very willingness to use sex as an adjunct to the sale of soap and automobiles may bear witness to our desire to make sexuality harmless by subduing it to the service of the market place. We have nominally liberalized our attitudes toward sex. Except for some survivals among inner-directed people who retain the stringent superego of earlier generations, sex expression has grown respectable. Men are supposed to be virile. Middle-class women are

[3] Pp. 29-30, Stendhal, *The Life of Henri Brulard,* New York, Vintage Books, 1955.

supposed to be sexually responsive, and even enterprising. Our vocabularies have become more forthright. Our behavior is looser, although not necessarily more relaxed. Almost every phase of sexual behavior is now used as raw material by our novelists. Few words or acts are forbidden to the playwright. Even the producers of American films are increasingly ready to treat the "facts of life" with something approaching reality.

Yet, although American society does seem to have freed itself from some inhibitions and restrictions which prevailed in the past, residues of that past continue to affect our attitudes toward sex. To be sure, it is currently admitted that sex is a normal, even a worthy part of life. But if one listens to the "experts" on sex or reads the books which they produce for the layman, one becomes aware that their treatment of the subject is so superficial that relatively few people have a true understanding of sex.

Thus, even today many laymen may be unpleasantly surprised to hear that sexuality does not begin just at adolescence. Study of the child and the adolescent has become one of the central concerns of American psychologists, social psychologists, and sociologists alike. (In passing, one might note that it was G. Stanley Hall, an American pioneer in the study of the adolescent and his psychology, who brought Freud to America to lecture in 1909.) They are aware of the increase in the anxieties which young people experience as they move into puberty and through adolescence; they accept the adolescent as a seeker for a place in the world; they recognize the difficulties experienced by adolescents in dealing with problems of acquiring sexual maturity.

All these problems are involved with the adolescent's underlying concern, the search for a viable self which Erik H. Erikson treats as the adolescent's special identity crisis.[4] Youth faces such crises in all societies, of course, but meeting them is especially difficult in societies changing as rapidly

[4] See *Childhood and Society*, New York, W. W. Norton & Co., 1955 and *Young Man Luther*, New York, W. W. Norton & Co., 1958.

as ours does. When Paul Goodman describes the state of *Growing Up Absurd*, he is concerned with the entire range of adolescent problems, but our dynamic society makes accommodation to sexual roles almost more difficult for young people than finding and carrying through vocational choices. Bruno Bettelheim, for example, thus sums up the differences between the sexual attitudes and prospects people face in our technological society and those which grow out of the experiences of people living in a less complex world:

> In societies in which technology has not yet affected the social conditions of women or their expectations, her sexual life is in far less conflict than in ours. It is still sufficient for her if her lover or husband enjoys sex with her. Since she feels that his enjoyment proves her a good woman, nothing stands in her way of enjoying herself; and, not worrying about whether she is frigid or has an orgastic experience, as likely as not she experiences orgasm. He, not obliged by older tradition or by any newer understanding to provide her with an orgastic experience, can enjoy himself, experience orgasm, and thus help her to experience it herself.
>
> In our society, the male youth needs as much as ever to have his virility attested by his sexual partner, and the female youth has a parallel need. But by now, the boy also needs to have his girl prove him a man by her so-called "orgastic experience," and the girl is even worse off. She not only has to prove him a man by making him experience orgasm; she must also prove her femininity by the same experience, because otherwise she must fear she is frigid. Sexual intercourse cannot often stand up to such complex emotional demands of proving so many things in addition to being enjoyable.[5]

Since the external conditions of people's lives are so different from what they were in Freud's day, it is not unreasonable that psychotherapists should encounter today different problems with patients from those with which they would have dealt in Freud's time. The therapist still needs to be fully acquainted with the dynamics of sexual development, and Freud still offers the best description and analysis

[5] Bruno Bettelheim, "The Problem of Generations," *Daedalus*, Winter 1962.

of those dynamics. Everyone who deals with young people —teachers, parents, social workers, administrators—or who wishes to increase his understanding of their elders (including himself) should also be familiar with Freud's analysis.

As previously mentioned, Freud's fundamental discoveries about sex have been emasculated. Although psychoanalysis has won particularly wide acceptance in the United States, that acceptance has come only as Freud's pessimism and his stress on libido theory have been de-emphasized, if not repudiated by the neo-Freudian groups, including the new Existentialist school of psychotherapy. The rigid severity of Freud's concepts, his uncompromising readiness to follow them through to their logical conclusion, have been peculiarly disturbing to Americans. Dissatisfaction with the character of American civilization was limited to a few intellectuals in the prosperous 1920's. Then economic depression and war further tended to suppress Americans' willingness to face up to the dark message which was implicit in Freud's theory. As Jean-Paul Sartre writes:

> It is childhood which traces out the blind alleys for prejudice; it is childhood which, feeling the curbs of its training, bucks like a snaffled colt and begins to resent belonging to a milieu. Today, psychoanalysis alone allows study to be made in depth of the process by which the child gropes his way in the dark and tries to act out, though he does not understand it, the social character which adults impose on him. It is psychoanalysis which shows if he is stifled in his role, whether he is trying to evade it or to assimilate himself completely to it. It is psychoanalysis alone that allows us to rediscover the whole man in the adult, that is to say, permits us to recognize not only his present determinations but also the burden of his life-history.[6] . . . Certainly, for the majority of us, our prejudices, our viewpoints, our beliefs are "dead-ends" *because they were first experienced in childhood.* It is our childish blindness, our protracted daze which accounts, in part, for our irrational reactions, the resistance we set up to reason. After all, just what was this fixation-making childhood if not a particular way of living the general interests of one's circle?[7]

[6] P. 46, Jean-Paul Sartre, *Critique de la raison dialectique*, I, Paris, Gallimard, 1960.

[7] P. 49, *ibid.* (Sartre's italics).

But modern Americans are committed to the belief that all things are possible, including escape from childhood. Many of them still believe that the child is a reservoir of goodness rather than an example of polymorphous sexual perversity. Hence, although Americans were quite prompt to see the potential usefulness of psychoanalytic treatment, they preferred other, more American-oriented theories—Rogers' client-centered therapy is a case in point. The growth of supportive and counseling therapy, the appeal of group psychotherapy, and the acceptance of selected portions of psychoanalytic ideas by many clergymen also indicate the kind of dilution which made Freud acceptable to a broad American public.

Most of these approaches, it should be repeated, de-emphasize sex, and particularly the influence of infantile sexuality. In his introduction to the first American translation of *Three Contributions to the Theory of Sex* (1910), Professor James Putnam pointed out the hostile attitude of his contemporaries toward the study of sexual behavior. Fifty years later, one must recognize that regardless of the impact of psychoanalytic thinking and despite the sexual sophistication to which many Americans dutifully pretend, a presumably informed public is still reluctant to approach problems of sexual behavior forthrightly and sensibly. Frank discussions of the nature and origin of sexual aberrations are still taboo although there is a market for sensationalism and superficiality. Psychotherapists find an appalling ignorance about sexual deviations, and social scientists see this ignorance reflected in outbreaks of public hysteria. "Sex Fiend" in a headline sells papers, however mild the story inside; and even somber classics of fiction are made saleable by "sexy" covers. The continued equation of sex with the forbidden and the dirty among so large a portion of the public leads one to think that the insights into the sexual behavior of man which Freud presented in these three essays and in his other writings are either not generally accepted or are badly misunderstood. The absence of serious sociological inquiry into variations from normal sexual behavior, and especially the lack of responsible original sociological studies on homosexuality, for example, offer an interesting sidelight on the failure of social scientists to broaden their understanding of changes in the American character during recent decades.

These observations, incidentally, do not imply any denigration of post-Freudian psychoanalytic theory. On the contrary, Hartmann's ego-psychology, Anna Freud's theory of the defense mechanisms, Fromm's cultural approach to the interpretation of psychoanalysis, and the insights of the Existentialist school all contribute significantly to a clearer understanding of the dynamics of neurosis and the requirements for its successful treatment. It is not easy to comprehend the so-called widening gap between what may be called "orthodox" Freudian theory and the modifications made by the "cultural" school. Both patients and psychoanalysts would benefit if greater emphasis were placed on the elements common to the theories of the principal psychoanalytic schools and less stress were put on their points of difference and divergence.

At the end of the first of the three essays reprinted here, Freud says:

> "If we are led to suppose that neurotics conserve the infantile state of their sexuality or return to it, our interest must then turn to the sexual life of the child, and we will then follow the play of influences which control the processes of development of the infantile sexuality up to its termination in a perversion, a neurosis or a normal sexual life."[8]

The newer psychoanalytic schools, however, have tended to de-emphasize the role of infantile sexuality. And both theory and patients have suffered as a result. Certainly, in a rapidly growing society, where the individual must play more complex roles, and roles for which he is often exceedingly ill-prepared, a fresh orientation toward therapy may be needed in order to help patients handle the problems which face them. Society does indeed change the patient. Undoubtedly, the character of the symptoms from which contemporary patients suffer does differ from those which Freud found in the

[8] P. 34, Sigmund Freud, *Three Contributions to the Theory of Sex.*

people who came to him for treatment. Many cases may not even be "clear-cut" in terms of their psychodynamics. Borderline cases seem on the increase; borderline treatment, new orientations in therapy, new modifications of the relationship between patient and analyst may be necessary therefore.

Nevertheless, this does not diminish the significance of Freud's original observations on the libido theory, for example. Those who reject that, offer no adequate substitute. Nor has any significent new theory on the development of sexuality been produced since Freud presented the basic concepts published here.

Similarly, although such studies as the Kinsey reports on sexual behavior and Irving Bieber's recent account of homosexuality[9] indicate that variations from conventionally acceptable sexual practices continue to play an important role in the lives of modern people, such studies of a strictly factual sort represent small progress in the theory of sexuality. And, indeed, even in the area of factual case study, we have not outmoded the basic nineteenth-century work of Krafft-Ebing *(Psychopathia Sexualis)*, Hirschfeld *(Sexual Anomalies and Perversions)*, and even Havelock Ellis *(The Psychology of Sex)*, all of whom discussed sexual deviation in what was presumably a more prudish age.

Freud's own discussion of such aberrations as fetichism, sadism, and masochism is still of fundamental importance: "Fetichism" (1927), "'A Child is Being Beaten,' A Contribution to the Study of the Origin of Sexual Perversions" (1919), and "The Economic Problem in Masochism" (1924) are all classics. His treatment of male homosexuality may not be the final word on the subject. The observations which Sullivan, Horney, and Bychowsky have made on homosexuality certainly should not be ignored. The absence of significant large-scale work on the etiology and treatment of homosexuality makes one wonder whether Freud and his contemporaries were not closer to a definitive interpretation of this phenomenon than are the modern analysts who stress the role of culture in its genesis. Freud's observations are still

[9] Irving Bieber *et al, Homosexuality: A Psychoanalytic Study*, New York, Basic Books, 1962.

as relevant today as they were when first set down in these essays. In cases of *inversion,* as Freud called homosexuality, the individuals concerned have experienced a very early stage of fixation on their mothers and subsequently identified with them. This formulation of Freud still serves psychotherapists in dealing with homosexual patients and in interpreting homosexual problems.

Cultural conditions may indeed change and therefore significantly affect the sexual roles and expectations which people experience. But the sexual impulse and its varied implications, as sketched by Freud in these essays, remain the same. This stress on the stability of sexual instincts may have confused and repelled many culturally oriented analysts during the last decades. They have undoubtedly detected the impacts of modern social and cultural changes upon both the adolescent and the adult, but in focusing upon these changes and in using them as the pivot about which to orient treatment, the culturalists have tended to ignore the basic dynamics which Freud discusses here.

It is this error which the reissue of *Three Contributions to the Theory of Sex* tries to correct. By becoming familiar with these essays, the lay reader may learn the differences between the superficial notions about Freud's concepts of sexuality to which he has been exposed and the reality of those concepts as Freud set them down. Through familiarity with those concepts, the reader may become more understanding of himself and of others as well. For many decades, Freud's work has been a source of stimulation to the social scientist. Fresh reading of this basic inquiry will show that the source is not exhausted.

HENDRIK M. RUITENBEEK*

New York City, April, 1962

* Dr. Ruitenbeek is a practicing psychotherapist in New York City and editor of two anthologies, *Psychoanalysis and Social Science* and *Psychoanalysis and Existential Philosophy.* Two new anthologies by Dr. Ruitenbeek, *Varieties of Classic Social Theory* and *The Condition of Man in Modern Society,* will be published in the near future.

Contents

Author's Prefaces

PREFACE TO THE SECOND EDITION

Although the author is fully aware of the gaps and obscurities contained in this small volume, he has, nevertheless, resisted a temptation to add to it the results obtained from the investigations of the last five years, fearing that thus its unified and documentary character would be destroyed. He accordingly reproduces the original text with but slight modifications, contenting himself with the addition of a few footnotes. For the rest, it is his ardent wish that this book may speedily become antiquated—to the end that the new material brought forward in it may be universally accepted, while the shortcomings it displays may give place to juster views.

Vienna, December, 1909

PREFACE TO THE THIRD EDITION

After watching for ten years the reception accorded to this book and the effect it has produced, I wish to provide the third edition of it with some prefatory remarks dealing with the misunderstandings of the book and the demands, insusceptible of fulfillment, made against it. Let me emphasize in the first place that whatever is here presented is derived entirely from everyday medical experience which is to be made more profound and scientifically important through the results of psychoanalytic investigation. The *Three Contributions to the Theory of Sex* can contain nothing except what psychoanalysis obliges them to accept or what it succeeds in corroborating. It is therefore excluded that they should ever be developed into a "theory of sex," and it is also quite intelligible that they will assume no attitude at all toward some important problems of the sexual life. This should not, however, give the impression that these omitted chapters of the great theme were unfamiliar to the author or that they were neglected by him as something of secondary importance.

The dependence of this work on the psychoanalytic experiences which have determined the writing of it shows itself not only in the selection but also in the arrangement of the material. A certain succession of stages was observed, the occasional factors are rendered prominent, the constitutional ones are left in the background, and the ontogenetic development receives greater consideration than the phylogenetic. For the occasional factors play the principal role in analysis, and are almost completely worked up in it, while the constitutional factors only become evident from behind as elements which have been made functional through experience, and a discussion of these would lead far beyond the working sphere of psychoanalysis.

A similar connection determines the relation between ontogenesis and phylogenesis. Ontogenesis may be considered as a repetition of phylogenesis insofar as the latter has not been varied by a more recent experience. The phylogenetic disposition makes itself visible behind the ontogenetic process. But fundamentally the constitution is really the precipitate of a former experience of the species to which the newer experience of the individual being is added as the sum of the occasional factors.

Beside its thoroughgoing dependence on psychoanalytic investigation I must emphasize as a character of this work of mine its intentional independence of biological investigation. I have carefully avoided the inclusion of the results of scientific investigation in general sex biology or of particular species of animals in this study of human sexual functions which is made possible by the technique of psychoanalysis. My aim was indeed to find out how much of the biology of the sexual life of man can be discovered by means of psychological investigation; I was able to point to additions and agreements which resulted from this examination, but I did not have to become confused if the psychoanalytic methods led in some points to views and results which deviated considerably from those merely based on biology.

I have added many passages in this edition, but I have abstained from calling attention to them, as in former editions, by special marks. The scientific work in our sphere has at present been retarded in its progress; nevertheless some supplements to this work were indispensable if it was to remain in touch with our newer psychoanalytic literature.

Vienna, October, 1914

PREFACE TO THE FOURTH EDITION[1]

Now that the floods of wartime have subsided, one may state with satisfaction that the interest in psychoanalytic research has remained unharmed in the great world. Yet not all parts of the doctrine have met with the same fate. The purely psychological declarations and discoveries of psychoanalysis concerning the unconscious, repression, the conflict which leads to illness, the advantage gained by illness, the mechanisms of symptom formation, and so on, enjoy growing recognition and find consideration even with opponents who are such on principle. That portion of the theory which borders upon biology, the basis of which is given in this small work, continues to call forth undiminished opposition and has even moved persons who had for a time occupied themselves intensively with psychoanalysis to turn away from it and to adopt new conceptions through which the role of the sexual factor for the normal and the pathological psychic life should be again restricted.

I cannot, however, bring myself to believe that this portion of the psychoanalytic doctrine could be so much further removed from the reality to be divined than the other parts. Memory and constantly repeated investigation tell me that it has originated from just as careful and unprejudiced observation and that this dissociation of the sexual theories in public recognition is not difficult to explain. In the first place, only those investigators are able to confirm the beginnings of human sexual life here described who possess sufficient patience and technical skill to carry the analysis forward into the patient's earliest childhood. The possibility for this is often lack-

[1] Reprinted in Fifth and Sixth German editions, 1922 and 1926 respectively, and in the definitive *Gesammelte Schriften*, Vol. V.

ing inasmuch as medical treatment desires a seemingly quicker discharge of the case. But persons other than physicians who are practicing psychoanalysis have no access at all to this field and no opportunity to form for themselves a judgment which would be uninfluenced by their own repugnances and prejudices. Had mankind known how to learn from direct observation of children, then these three contributions might have remained wholly unwritten.

Moreover, it must be remembered that some of the ideas in this work, namely, the emphasizing of the importance of the sexual life in all human achievements and the extension of the concept of sexuality attempted here, have always furnished the strongest motives for the resistance against psychoanalysis. In their desire for a resounding slogan some have gone so far as to speak of "pansexualism" of psychoanalysis, and to hurl at it the senseless reproach that it explains "everything" through sexuality. One would wonder at this were one able to forget altogether the confusing and forgettable effect of affective factors. For, quite some time ago, the philosopher Arthur Schopenhauer had already upbraided man with the degree in which his actions and thoughts are determined by sexual strivings—in the usual sense of the word—and one could expect that a world of readers would have been unable to drive so impressive a reminder completely from memory! But as to the "extension" of the idea of sexuality, which becomes necessary through the analysis of children and of so-called perverts, may all those who from their exalted standpoint look down scornfully upon psychoanalysis remember how closely the extended sexuality of psychoanalysis corresponds with the Eros of the divine Plato. (See Nachmansohn, "Freud's Libidotheorie verglichen mit der Eroslehre Platos," *Inter. Zeitschr. f. Psychoanalyse*, III, 1915.)

Vienna, May, 1920

Foreword

The somewhat famous *Three Contributions*, which Dr. Brill is here bringing to the attention of an English-reading public, occupies—brief as it is—an important position among the achievements of its author, a great investigator and pioneer in an important line. It is not claimed that the facts here gathered are altogether new. The subject of the sexual instinct and its aberrations has long been before the scientific world, and the names of many effective toilers in this vast field are known to every student. When one passes beyond the strict domains of science and considers what is reported of the sexual life in folkways and art lore and the history of primitive culture and in romance, the sources of information are immense. Freud has made considerable additions to this stock of knowledge, but he has also done something of far greater consequence than this. He has worked out, with incredible penetration, the part which this instinct plays in every phase of human life and in the development of human character, and has been able to establish on a firm footing the remarkable thesis that psychoneurotic illnesses never occur with a perfectly normal sexual life. Other sorts of emotions contribute to the result, but some aberration of the sexual life is always present, as the cause of especially insistent emotions and repressions.

The instincts with which every child is born furnish desires or cravings which must be dealt with in some fashion. They may be refined ("sublimated"), so far as is necessary and desirable, into energies of other sorts—as happens readily with the play instinct—or they may remain as the source of perversions and inversions, and of cravings of new sorts substituted for those of the more primitive kinds under the pressure of a conventional civilization. The symptoms of the functional psychoneuroses represent, after a fashion, some of these distorted attempts to find a substitute for the imperative cravings born of the sexual instincts, and their form often depends, in part at least, on the peculiarities of the sexual life in infancy and early childhood. It is Freud's service to have investigated this inadequately chronicled period of existence with extraordinary acumen. In so doing, he made it plain that the "perversions" and "inversions," which reappear later under such striking shapes, belong to the normal sexual life of the young child and are seen, in veiled forms, in almost every case of nervous illness.

It cannot too often be repeated that these discoveries represent no fanciful deductions, but are the outcome of rigidly careful observations which anyone who will sufficiently prepare himself can verify. Critics fret over the amount of "sexuality" that Freud finds evidence of in the histories of his patients, and assume that he puts it there. But such criticisms are evidences of misunderstandings and proofs of ignorance.

Freud had learned that the amnesias of hypnosis and of hysteria were not absolute but relative and that in covering the lost memories, much more, of unexpected sort, was often found. Others, too, had gone as far as this, and stopped. But this investigator determined that nothing but the absolute impossibility of going further should make him cease from urging his patients into an inexorable scrutiny of the unconscious regions of their memories and thoughts, such as never had been made before. Every species of forgetfulness, even the forgetfulness of childhood's years, was made to yield its hidden stores of knowledge; dreams, even though apparently absurd, were found to be interpreters of a varied class of thoughts, active, although repressed as out of harmony with the selected life of consciousness; layer after layer, new sets of motives underlying motives were laid bare, and each patient's interest was strongly enlisted in the task of learning to know himself in order more truly and wisely to "sublimate" himself. Gradually other workers joined patiently in this laborious undertaking, which now stands, for those who have taken pains to comprehend it, as by far the most important movement in psychopathology.

It must, however, be recognized that these essays, of which Dr. Brill has given a translation that cannot but be timely, concern a subect which is not only important but unpopular. Few physicians read the works of v. Krafft-Ebing, Magnus Hirschfield, Albert Moll, and others of like sort. The remarkable volumes of Havelock Ellis were refused publication in his native England. The sentiments which inspired this hostile attitude toward the study of the sexual life are still active, though growing steadily less common. One may easily believe that if the facts which Freud's truth-seeking researches forced him to recognize and to publish had not been of an unpopular sort, his rich and abundant contributions to observational psychology, to the significance of dreams, to the etiology and therapeutics of the psychoneuroses, to the interpretation of mythology, would have won for him, by universal acclaim, the same recognition among all physicians that he has received from a rapidly increasing band of followers and colleagues.

May Dr. Brill's translation help toward this end.

There are two further points on which some comments should be made. The first is this, that those who conscientiously desire to learn all that they can from Freud's remarkable contributions should not be content to read any one of them alone. His various publications, such as *The Selected Papers on Hysteria and Other Psychoneuroses*,[1] *The Interpretation of Dreams*,[2] *The Psychopathology of Everyday Life*,[3] *Wit and Its Relation to the Unconscious*,[4] the analysis of the case of the little boy called Hans, the study of Leonardo da Vinci,[5] and the various short essays in the four *Sammlungen kleiner Schriften*, not only all hang together but also supplement each other to a remarkable extent. Unless a course of study such as this is undertaken, many critics may think various statements and inferences in this volume to be farfetched or find them too obscure for comprehension.[6]

The other point is the following: One frequently hears the

[1] Translated by A. A. Brill, Nervous and Mental Disease Monograph Series, No. 4.

[2] Translated by A. A. Brill (The Macmillan Co., New York, and Allen & Unwin, London).

[3] Translated by A. A. Brill (The Macmillan Co., New York).

[4] Translated by A. A. Brill (Dodd, Mead & Co., New York).

[5] Translated by A. A. Brill (Dodd, Mead & Co., New York).

[6] Freud's "collected works" *(Gesammelte Schriften)* are now available in German in twelve volumes. Many of the studies are in individual translations, and the International Psychoanalytic Library

psychoanalytic method referred to as if it were customary for those practicing it to exploit the sexual experiences of their patients and nothing more, and the insistence on the details of the sexual life, presented in this book, is likely to emphasize that notion. But the fact is, as every thoughtful inquirer is aware, that the whole progress of civilization, whether in the individual or the race, consists largely in a "sublimation" of infantile instincts, and especially certain portions of the sexual instinct, to ends other than those they seemed designed to serve. Art and poetry are fed on this fuel, and the evolution of character and mental force is largely of the same origin. All the forms which this sublimation, or the abortive attempts at sublimation, may take in any given case should come out in the course of a thorough psychoanalysis. It is not the sexual life alone, but every interest and every motive, that must be inquired into by the physician who is seeking to obtain all the data about the patient necessary for his reeducation and his cure. But all the thoughts and emotions and desires and motives which appear in the man or woman of adult years were once crudely represented in the obscure instincts of the infant, and among these instincts those which were concerned directly or indirectly with the sexual emotions, in a wide sense, are certain to be found in every case to have been the most important for the end result.

JAMES J. PUTNAM

Boston, August 23, 1910

---

has published four volumes in England of many important papers. For Freudian literature up to 1926, see Rickman, *Index Psychoanalyticus* (International Psychoanalytic Library, No. 14, London, 1928). For later literature see *Psychoanalytic Review*, published quarterly.

Translator's Foreword

This small but most important volume of Professor Freud enjoys the distinction of having evoked almost as much controversy and irritation as did the revolutionary theories of Darwin. However, not even idyllic Christianity was born in peace; irritation seems to be biologically necessary and even salutary, especially to those who are snugly entrenched in their protective academic cathedrals. It is, therefore, pleasing to state that, with the exception of those who fled precipitously at the first impact with this small volume and who have since then been fed on an emasculated psychoanalysis purveyed by a handful of psychology specialists, the others have gradually become acclimated to its truths. But what is of particular significance to us is that even those of the former group who may still be counted among Professor Freud's opponents are, in spite of themselves, talking and writing about the sex life of their patients. Times have really changed, sexually speaking, since this work made its first English appearance back in 1910.[1] The hypocritical reserve so widely prevalent thirty or even twenty years ago may still be lingering in the remote mountain fastnesses in some of the less civilized nooks of our nation, but the scientific and more liberal-minded people of metropolitan regions are becoming distinctly more honest and outspoken in their attitude to sex. In psychiatric circles, it is also refreshing to note that the younger generation, following the leadership of Professor Bleuler, is fearlessly investigating the role of sex in their patients' psyche, only to be increasingly convinced of its importance. Thus Freud's dictum that no neurosis is possible in a normal sexual life has weathered the raging storms of more than a quarter of a century of criticism and has stood all tests firmly.

As a textbook of psychosexuality, this book is unique. For

[1] German original appeared in 1905, published by Deuticke.

unlike other works on sex it is of interest not only to the student of abnormal manifestations to whom it reveals the mechanisms of infantile sexuality, perversions, and their relation to the neuroses; but in addition, by giving a systematic and integrated account of the whole psychosexual development of man, it becomes indispensable to the psychologist, the anthropologist, sociologist, the jurist, and above all the teacher.

The translation of this edition follows the original text as it now appears in Professor Freud's *Collected Papers*.[2]

A. A. BRILL

[2] Freud, *Gesammelte Schriften*, Vol. V (Internationaler Psychoanalytischer Verlag, Leipzig, Wien u. Zurich, 1924).

Three Contributions to the Theory of Sex

Contribution I

THE SEXUAL ABERRATIONS[1] [7] *

The fact of sexual need in man and animal is expressed in biology by the assumption of a "sexual instinct." This impulse is made analogous to the impulse of taking nourishment, and to hunger. The sexual expression corresponding to hunger not being found colloquially, science uses the expression "libido."[2]

Popular conception makes definite assumptions concerning the nature and qualities of this sexual impulse. It is supposed to be absent during childhood and to commence about the time of and in connection with the maturing process of puberty; it is supposed that it manifests itself in irresistible attractions exerted by one sex upon the other and that its aim is sexual union or at least such actions as would lead to union.

But we have every reason to see in these assumptions a very untrustworthy picture of reality. On closer examination they are [8] found to abound in errors, inaccuracies, and hasty conclusions.

If we introduce two terms and call the person from whom the sexual attraction emanates the *sexual object*, and the ac-

[1] The facts contained in the first "Contribution" have been gathered from the familiar publications of Krafft-Ebing, Moll, Moebius, Havelock Ellis, Schrenk-Notzing, Löwenfeld, Eulenberg, I. Bloch, and M. Hirschfeld, and from the later works published in the *Jahrbuch für sexuelle Zwischenstufen.* As these publications also mention the other literature bearing on this subject, I may forbear giving detailed references.

The conclusions reached through the psychoanalytic investigation of sexual inverts are all based on the reports of J. Sadger and on my own experience.

* Figures in brackets [ ] indicate pages in the *Gesammelte Schriften,* Vol. 5, with which pagination the Sixth Edition (Deuticke), 1925–1926, here followed, is identical.

[2] The single adequate or fitting word of the German language, *Lust,* unfortunately has many meanings, and signifies the sensation of needs as well as that of satisfaction. For general use the word "libido" is best translated by "craving" (Prof. James J. Putnam, *Journal of Abnormal Psychology,* Vol. IV, 6).

tion towarl which the impulse strives the *sexual aim,* then the scientifically examined experience shows us many deviations in reference to both sexual object and sexual aim, the relations of which to the accepted standard require thorough investigation.

1. DEVIATION IN REFERENCE TO THE SEXUAL OBJECT

The popular theory of the sexual impulse corresponds closely to the poetic fable of dividing the person into two halves—man and woman—who strive to become reunited through love. It is therefore very surprising to hear that there are men for whom the sexual object is not woman but man and that there are women for whom it is not man but woman. Such *persons* are called contrary sexuals, or better, inverts; the *condition,* that of inversion. The number of such individuals is considerable though difficult of accurate determination.[3]

A. Inversion

THE BEHAVIOR OF INVERTS. The above-mentioned persons behave in many ways quite differently.

(*a*) They are absolutely inverted; that is, their sexual object must be always of the same sex, while the opposite sex can never be to them an object of sexual longing, but leaves them indifferent or [9] may even evoke sexual repugnance. As men they are unable, on account of this repugnance, to perform the normal sexual act or miss all pleasure in its performance.

(*b*) They are amphigenously inverted (psychosexually hermaphroditic); that is, their sexual object may belong indifferently to either the same or to the other sex. The inversion lacks the character of exclusiveness.

(*c*) They are occasionally inverted; that is, under certain external conditions, chief among which are the inaccessibility of the normal sexual objection and imitation, they are able to

[3] For the difficulties entailed in the attempt to ascertain the proportional number of inverts, compare the word of M. Hirschfeld in the *Jahrbuch für sexuelle Zwischenstufen,* 1904. (Cf. also Brill, "The Conception of Homosexuality," *Journal of the A.M.A.,* August 2, 1913.)

take as the sexual object a person of the same sex and thus find sexual gratification.

The inverted also manifest a manifold behavior in their judgment about the peculiarities of their sexual impulse. Some take the inversion as a matter of course, just as the normal person does regarding his libido, firmly demanding the same rights as the normal. Others, however, strive against the fact of their inversion and perceive in it a morbid compulsion.[4]

Other variations concern the relations of time. The characteristics of the inversion in any individual may date back as far as his memory goes, or they may become manifest to him at a definite period before or after puberty.[5] The character is either retained throughout life, or it occasionally recedes or represents an episode on the road to normal development. [10] A periodical fluctuation between the normal and the inverted sexual object has also been observed. Of special interest are those cases in which the libido changes, taking on the character of inversion after a painful experience with the normal sexual object.

These different categories of variation generally exist independently of one another. In the most extreme cases it can regularly be assumed that the inversion has existed at all times and that the person feels contented with his peculiar state.

Many authors will hesitate to gather into a unit all the cases enumerated here and will prefer to emphasize the differences rather than the common characters of these groups, a view which corresponds with their preferred judgment of inversions. But no matter what divisions may be set up, it cannot be overlooked that all transitions are abundantly met with, so that the formation of a series would seem to impose itself.

CONCEPTION OF INVERSION. The first attention bestowed upon inversion gave rise to the conception that it was a con-

[4] Such a striving against the compulsion to inversion favors influence by suggestion or psychoanalysis.

[5] Many have justly emphasized the fact that the autobiographic statements of inverts, as to the time of the appearance of their tendency to inversion, are untrustworthy, as they may have repressed from memory any evidences of heterosexual feelings. Psychoanalysis has confirmed this suspicion in all cases of inversion accessible, and has decidedly changed their anamnesis by filling up the infantile amnesias.

genital sign of nervous degeneration. This harmonized with the fact that doctors first met it among the nervous, or among persons giving such an impression. There are two elements which should be considered independently in this conception: the congenitality and the degeneration.

DEGENERATION. This term "degeneration" is open to the objections which may be urged against the promiscuous use of this word in general. It has in fact become customary to designate all morbid manifestations not of traumatic or infectious origin as degenerative. Indeed, Magnan's classification of degenerates makes it possible that the highest general configuration of [11] nervous accomplishment need not exclude the application of the concept of degeneration. Under the circumstances, it is a queston what use and what new content the judgment of "degeneration" still possesses. It would seem more appropriate not to speak of degeneration: (1) where there are not many marked deviations from the normal; (2) where the capacity for working and living do not in general appear markedly impaired.[6]

That the inverted are not degenerates in this qualified sense can be seen from the following facts:

1. The inversion is found among persons who otherwise show no marked deviation from the normal.

2. It is found also among persons whose capabilities are not disturbed and who, on the contrary, are distinguished by especially high intellectual development and ethical culture.[7]

3. If one disregards the patients of one's own practice and strives to comprehend a wider field of experience, he will in two directions encounter facts which will prevent him from assuming inversions as a degenerative sign.

[6] With what reserve the diagnosis of degeneration should be made and what slight practical significance can be attributed to it can be gathered from the discussions of Moebius (*Ueber Entartung: Grenzfragen des Nerven- und Seelenlebens*, No. III, 1900). He says: "If we review the wide sphere of degeneration upon which we have here turned some light, we can conclude without further ado that it is really of little value to diagnose degeneration."

[7] We must agree with the spokesman of "Uranism" (I. Bloch) that some of the most prominent men known have been inverts and perhaps absolute inverts.

(*a*) It must be considered that inversion was a frequent manifestation among the ancient nations at the height of their culture. It was an institution endowed with important functions. (*b*) It is found to be unusually prevalent among savages and primitive races, whereas the term "degeneration" is generally limited to higher [12] civilization (I. Bloch). Even among the most civilized nations of Europe, climate and race have a most powerful influence on the distribution of, and attitude toward, inversion.[8]

INNATENESS. Only for the first and most extreme class of inverts, as can be imagined, has innateness been claimed, and this from their own assurance that at no time in their life has their sexual impulse followed a different course. The fact of the existence of two other classes, especially of the third, is difficult to reconcile with the assumption of its being congenital. Hence, the propensity of those holding this view to separate the group of absolute inverts from the others results in the abandonment of the general conception of inversion. Accordingly, in a number of cases the inversion would be of a congenital character, while in others it might originate from other causes.

In contradistinction to this conception is that which assumes inversion to be an *acquired* character of the sexual impulse. It is based on the following facts:

(1) In many inverts (even absolute ones) an early affective sexual impression can be demonstrated, as a result of which the homosexual inclination developed.

(2) In many others outer influences of a promoting and inhibiting nature can be demonstrated, which in earlier or later life led to a fixation of the inversion—among which are exclusive relations with the same sex, companionship in war, detention in prison, dangers of heterosexual intercourse, celibacy, genital weakness, and so on. [13]

(3) Hypnotic suggestion may remove the inversion, which would be surprising if it were of a congenital character.

[8] In the conception of inversion the pathological features have been separated from the anthropological. For this credit is due to I. Bloch (*Beiträge zur Ätiologie der Psychopathia Sexualis,* 2 Teile, 1902–1903), who has also brought into prominence the existence of inversion in the old civilized nations.

In view of all this, the existence of congenital inversion can certainly be questioned. The objection may be made to it that a more accurate examination of those claimed to be congenitally inverted will probably show that the direction of the libido was determined by a definite experience of early childhood, which has not been retained in the conscious memory of the person but which can be brought back to memory by proper influences (Havelock Ellis). According to this author inversion can be designated only as a frequent variation of the sexual impulse which may be determined by a number of external circumstances of life.

The apparent certainty thus reached is, however, overthrown by the retort that manifestly there are many persons who have experienced even in their early youth those very sexual influences such as seduction, mutual onanism, without becoming inverts, or without constantly remaining so. Hence, one is forced to assume that the alternatives congenital and acquired are either incomplete or do not cover the circumstances present in inversions.

EXPLANATION OF INVERSION. The nature of inversion is explained neither by the assumption that it is congenital nor that it is acquired. In the first case, we need to be told what there is in it of the congenital, unless we are satisfied with the roughest explanation, namely, that a person brings along a congenital sexual impulse connected with a definite sexual object. In the second case it is a question whether the manifold accidental influences suffice to explain the acquisition unless there is something in the individual to meet them halfway. The negation of this last factor is inadmissible according to our former conclusions. [14]

THE APPROACH TO INVERSION. Since the time of Frank Lydston, Kiernan, and Chevalier, a new series of ideas has been introduced for the explanation of the possibility of sexual inversion. These contain a new contradiction to the popular belief which assumes that a human being is either a man or a woman. Science shows cases, however, in which the sexual characteristics appear blurred and thus the sexual distinction is made difficult, especially on an anatomical basis. The genitals of such persons unite the male and female characteristics (hermaphroditism). In rare cases both parts of the sexual apparatus are well developed (true hermaphroditism), but usually both are stunted.[9]

The importance of these abnormalities lies in the fact that they unexpectedly facilitate the understanding of the normal formation. A certain degree of anatomical hermaphroditism really belongs to the normal. In no normally formed male or female are traces of the apparatus of the other sex lacking; these either continue functionless as rudimentary organs, or they are transformed for the purpose of assuming other functions.

The conception which we gather from this long-known anatomical fact is the original predisposition to bisexuality, which in the course of development has changed to monosexuality, leaving slight remnants of the stunted sex.

It was natural to transfer this conception to the psychic sphere and to conceive the inversion in its aberrations as an expression of psychic hermaphroditism. In order to bring the question to a decision, it was necessary to have only one other circumstance, namely, a regular concurrence of the inversion with the psychic and somatic signs of hermaphroditism. [15]

But this second expectation was not realized. The relations between the assumed psychical and the demonstrable anatomical androgyny should never be conceived as being so close. There is frequently found in the inverted a diminution of the sexual impulse (H. Ellis) and a slight anatomical stunting of the organs. This, however, is found frequently but by no means regularly or preponderantly. Thus we must recognize that inversion and somatic hermaphroditism are totally independent of each other.

Great importance has also been attached to the so-called secondary and tertiary sex characters, and their aggregate occurrence in the inverted has been emphasized (H. Ellis). There is much truth in this, but it should not be forgotten that the secondary and tertiary sex characteristics very frequently

[9] Compare the last detailed discussion of somatic hermaphroditism (Taruffi, *Hermaphroditismus und Zeugungsunfähigkeit*, German edit. by R. Teuscher, 1903), and the works of Neugebauer in many volumes of the *Jahrbuch für sexuelle Zwischenstufen*.

manifest themselves in the other sex, thus indicating androgyny without, however, involving changes in the sexual object in the sense of an inversion.

Psychic hermaphroditism would gain in substantiality if parallel with the inversion of the sexual object there should be at least a change in the other psychic qualities, such as in the impulses and distinguishing traits characteristic of the other sex. But such inversion of character can be expected with some regularity only in inverted women; in men the most perfect psychic manliness may be united with the inversion. If one firmly adheres to the hypothesis of a psychic hermaphroditism, one must add that in certain spheres its manifestations allow the recognition of only a very slight contrary determination. The same also holds true in the somatic androgyny. According to Halban, the appearance of individual stunted organs and secondary sex characters are quite independent of each other.[10] [16]

A spokesman of the masculine inverts stated the bisexual theory in its crudest form in the following words: "It is a female brain in a male body." But we do not know the characteristics of a "female brain." The substitution of the anatomical for the psychological is as frivolous as it is unjustified. The tentative explanation by v. Krafft-Ebing seems to be more precisely formulated than that of Ulrich but does not essentially differ from it. Krafft-Ebing thinks that the bisexual predisposition supplies the individual with male and female brain centers as well as with the somatic sexual organs. These centers develop first toward puberty mostly under the influence of the independent sex glands. We can, however, say the same of the male and female "centers" as of the male and female brains; and, moreover, we do not even know whether we can assume for the sexual functions separate brain locations ("centers") such as we may assume for language.

At all events, after this discussion two notions persist; first, that a bisexual predisposition is to be presumed for the inversion also; only, we do not know of what it consists beyond

[10] J. Halban, "Die Entstehung der Geschlechtscharaktere," *Arch. für Gynäkologie*, Bd. 70, 1903. See also there the literature on the subject.

the anatomical formations; and, second, that we are dealing with disturbances which are experienced by the sexual impulse during its development.[11] [17]

THE SEXUAL OBJECT OF THE INVERT. The theory of psychic hermaphroditism presupposed that the sexual object of the inverted is the reverse of the normal. The inverted man, like the woman, succumbs to the charms emanating from manly qualities of body and mind; he feels like a woman and seeks a man.

But however true this may be for a great number of inverts, it by no means indicates the general character of inversion. There is no doubt that a great part of the male inverted have retained the psychic character of virility, that proportionately they show but little of the secondary characters of the other

[11] According to a report in Vol. VI of the *Jahrbuch für sexuelle Zwischenstufen,* E. Gley is supposed to have been the first to mention bisexuality as an explanation of inversion. He published a paper ("Les abérrations de l'instinct sexuel") in the *Revue Philosophique* as early as January, 1884. It is, moreover, noteworthy that the majority of authors who trace inversion back to bisexuality assume this factor not only for the inverts but also for those who have developed normally, and justly interpret the inversion as a result of disturbance in development. Among these authors are Chevalier (*Inversion Sexuelle,* 1893) and v. Krafft-Ebing ("Zur Erklärung der konträren Sexualempfindung," *Jahrbücher für Psychiatrie u. Nervenheilkunde,* XIII), who states that there are a number of observations "from which at least the virtual and continued existence of this second center (of the underlying sex) results." A Dr. Arduin (*Die Frauenfrage und die sexuellen Zwischenstufen,* Vol. II of the *Jahrbuch für sexuelle Zwischenstufen,* 1900) states that "in every man there exist male and female elements." See also the same *Jahrbuch,* Bd. I, 1899 ("Die objektive Diagnose der Homosexualität," by Mr. Hirschfeld, pp. 8–9). In the determination of sex, as far as heterosexual persons are concerned, some are disproportionately more strongly developed than others. G. Herman is firm in his belief "that in every woman there are male and in every man there are female germs and qualities" ("Genesis, das Gesetz der Zeugung," Bd. IX, *Libido und Manie,* 1903). As recently as 1906 W. Fliess *(Der Ablauf des Lebens)* has claimed ownership of the idea of bisexuality (in the sense of double sex). In noninformed circles the assertion is made that the recently deceased philosopher O. Weininger is the authority for the human bisexuality conception, since this notion is made the foundation of his rather rash work (*Geschlecht und Charakter,* 1903 [translated into English]). The citations here made show how unfounded is such a claim.

sex, and that they really look for real feminine psychic features in their sexual object. If that were not so it would be incomprehensible why masculine prostitution, in offering itself to inverts, copies in all its exterior, today as in antiquity, the dress and attitudes of woman. This imitation would otherwise be an insult to the ideal of the inverts. Among the Greeks, where the most manly men were found among inverts, it is quite obvious that it was not the masculine character of the boy which kindled the love of man; it was his physical resemblance to woman as well as his feminine psychic qualities, such as shyness, demureness, and the need of instruction and help. As soon as the boy himself became a man he ceased to be a sexual object for men and in turn became a lover of boys. The sexual object in this case as in many others is therefore not of the like sex, but unites both sex characters, a compromise between the impulses striving for the man and for the woman, but firmly conditioned by the masculinity of body (the genitals).[12] [19]

[12] Although psychoanalysis has not yet given us a full explanation for the origin of inversion, it has revealed the psychic mechanism of its genesis and has essentially enriched the problems in question. In all the cases examined we have ascertained that the later inverts go through in their childhood a phase of very intense but short-lived fixation on the woman (usually on the mother), and after overcoming it they identify themselves with the woman and take themselves as the sexual object; that is, proceeding on a narcissistic basis, they look for young men resembling themselves in persons whom they wish to love as their mother has loved them. We have, moreover, frequently found that alleged inverts are by no means indifferent to the charms of women, but the excitation evoked by the woman is always transferred to a male object. They thus repeat through life the mechanism which gave origin to their inversion. Their obsessive striving for the man proves to be determined by their restless flight from the woman. Psychoanalytic research very strongly opposes the attempt to separate homosexuals from other persons as a group of a special nature. By also studying sexual excitations other than the manifestly open ones, it discovers that all men are capable of homosexual object selection and actually accomplish this in the unconscious. Indeed the attachments of libidinous feelings to persons of the same sex play no small role as factors in normal psychic life, and as causative factors of disease they play a greater role than those belonging to the opposite sex. According to psychoanalysis, it rather seems that it is the independence of the object, selection of the sex of the object, the same free disposal over male and female objects, as observed in childhood, in primitive states and in prehistoric times, which forms the origin

from which the normal as well as the inversion types developed, following restrictions in this or that direction. In the psychoanalytic sense the exclusive sexual interest of the man for the woman is also a problem requiring an explanation, and is not something that is self-evident and explainable on the basis of chemical attraction. The determination as to the definite sexual behavior does not occur until after puberty, and is the result of a series of as yet not observable factors, some of which are of a constitutional, while some are of an accidental, nature. Certainly some of these factors can turn out to be so enormous that by their character they influence the result. In general, however, the multiplicity of the determining factors is reflected by the manifoldness of the outcomes in the manifest sexual behavior of the person. In the inversion types it can be ascertained that they are altogether controlled by an archaic constitution and by primitive psychic mechanisms. The importance of the *narcissistic object selection* and the *clinging* to the erotic significance of the *anal* zone seem to be their most essential characteristics. But one gains nothing by separating the most extreme inversion types from the others on the basis of such constitutional peculiarities. What is found in the latter as seemingly an adequate determinant can also be demonstrated only in lesser force in the constitution of transitional types and in manifestly normal persons. The differences in the results may be of a qualitative nature, but analysis shows that the differences in the determinants are only quantitative. As a remarkable factor among the accidental influences of the object selection, we found the sexual rejection or the early sexual intimidation, and our attention was also called to the fact that the existence of both parents plays an important role in the child's life. The disappearance of a strong father in childhood not infrequently favors the inversion. Finally, one can put forth the claim that the inversion of the sexual object should notionally be strictly separated from the mixing of the sex characteristics in the subject. A certain degree of independence is unmistakable also in this relation. A series of important points of view concerning the question of inversion have been brought forward by Ferenczi (in a contribution, "Zur Nosologie der männlichen Homosexualität" [Homoerotic], in *Int. Zeit. f. Psa.*, II, 1914). Published in English in *Contribution to Psychoanalysis*, I (Bodger, Boston, 1916). Ferenczi correctly criticizes the fact that under the term Homosexuality (which term we would replace by the better one Homoerotic) a number of different conditions are grouped which are of quite variable significance both from an organic as well as from a psychical viewpoint because the one symptom of inversion is present. He shows that there are but four very marked differences at least between two types of subject-homoerotics, who feel and act like women, and the object-homoerotic who is masculine throughout and has only (mistakenly) exchanged a female object against one of the same sex. The first he recognizes as a true "intermediary sexual stage" in the sense of Magnus Hirschfeld; the second he terms—less fortunately—a compulsion neurotic. The striving against the tendency to inversion as well as the possibility of psychical influence is possible only with the object homoerotic. It may also be added that after the recognition of these two types in many indi-

The conditions in the woman are more definite; here the active inverts, with special frequency, show the somatic and psychic characters of man and desire femininity in their sexual object; though even here greater variation will be found on more intimate investigation.

THE SEXUAL AIM OF THE INVERT. The important fact to bear in mind is that no uniformity of the sexual aim can be attributed to inversion. Intercourse per anum in men by no means goes with inversion; masturbation is just as frequently the exclusive aim; and the limitation of the sexual aim to mere effusion of feelings is here even more frequent than in heterosexual love. [20] In women, too, the sexual aims of the inverted are manifest, among which contact with the mucous membrane of the mouth seems to be preferred.

CONCLUSION. Though from the material on hand we are by no means in a position to explain satisfactorily the origin

---

viduals a certain amount of subject homoeroticism is found mixed with a portion of object homoeroticism.

Of recent years biological workers, especially Eugen Steinach, have thrown a clear light upon the organic conditionings of homoerotism as well as upon sexual characters. Through the experimental procedure of castration followed by implanting the gonads of the opposite sex, he was able in different mammals to change males into females and vice versa. The change concerns more or less completely the somatic sexual characters and the psychosexual behavior (as subject- and object-erotic). The carriers of this sex-determining power are not that portion of the sexual glands which builds up the sexual cells but the so-called interstitial cells of the organs (the puberty glands).

In one case the sexual alteration took place in a man whose testicles had been damaged by tuberculosis. In his sexual life he had behaved as a passive homosexual woman, and showed very clearly marked secondary female sexual characters (hair distribution, nature of facial hair, fatty mammæ, and female hips). Following the implantation of a cryptorchids testicle, this man began to behave as a man and directed his libido toward the female in the normal manner. At the same time the somatic female sex character disappeared (A. Lipschütz, *Die Pubersätsdrüse und ihre Wirkungen* [Bern, 1919]).

It would be unjust to maintain that the knowledge of inversion is placed on a new basis, and premature to expect directly a way to the cure of homosexuality. W. Fliess has correctly accented the fact that this experimental experience does not solve the problem of the general bisexual anlage of the higher animals. It seems to me much more probable that a direct confirmation of the accepted bisexuality will come from such and further investigations.

of inversion, we can say that through this investigation we have obtained an insight which can become of greater significance to us than the solution of the above problem. Our attention is called to the fact that we have assumed a too close connection between the sexual impulse and the sexual object. The experience gained from the so-called abnormal cases teaches us that a connection exists between the sexual impulse and the sexual object which we are in danger of overlooking in the uniformity of normal [21] states where the impulse seems to bring with it the object. We are thus instructed to separate this connection between the impulse and the object. The sexual impulse is probably entirely independent of its object and is not originated by the stimuli proceeding from the object.

B. The Sexually Immature and Animals as Sexual Objects

Whereas those sexual inverts whose sexual object does not belong to the normally adapted sex appear to the observer as a collective number of perhap otherwise normal individuals, the persons who choose for their sexual object the sexually immature (children) arc apparently from the first sporadic aberrations. Only exceptionally are children the exclusive sexual objects. They are mostly drawn into this role by a faint-hearted and impotent individual who makes use of such substitutes, or when an impulsive, urgent desire cannot at the time secure the proper object. Still, it throws some light on the nature of the sexual impulse, that it should suffer such great variation and depreciation of its object, a thing which hunger, adhering more energetically to its object, would allow only in the most extreme cases. The same may be said of sexual relations with animals—a thing not at all rare among farmers—where the sexual attraction goes beyond the limits of the species.

For esthetic reasons one would like to attribute this and other excessive aberrations of the sexual impulse to the insane, but this cannot be done. Experience teaches that among the latter no disturbances of the sexual impulse can be found other than those observed among the sane, or among whole races and classes. Thus we find with gruesome frequency sexual abuse of children [22] by teachers and servants merely because they have the best opportunities for it. The psychotic present the aforesaid aberration only in a somewhat intensified form; or what is of special significance is the fact that the aberration becomes exclusive and takes the place of the normal sexual gratification.

This very remarkable relation of sexual variations ranging from the normal to the psychotic gives material for reflection. It seems to me that the fact to be explained would show that the impulses of the sexual life belong to those which even normally are most poorly controlled by the higher psychic activities. He who is in any way psychically abnormal, be it in social or ethical conditions, is, according to my experience, regularly so in his sexual life. But many are abnormal in their sexual life who in every other respect correspond to the average; they have followed the human cultural development, but sexuality remained as their weak point.

As a general result of these discussions we come to see that, under numerous conditions and among a surprising number of individuals, the nature and value of the sexual object steps into the background. There is something else in the sexual impulse which is the essential and constant.[13]

2. DEVIATION IN REFERENCE TO THE SEXUAL AIM

The union of the genitals in the characteristic act of copulation is taken as the normal sexual aim. It serves to loosen the sexual [23] tension and temporarily to quench the sexual desire (gratification analogous to satisfaction of hunger). Yet even in the most normal sexual process those additions are distinguishable, the development of which leads to the aberrations described as *perversions*. Thus certain intermediary relations to the sexual object connected with copulation, such as

[13] The most pronounced difference between the love life *(Liebesleben)* of antiquity and ours lies in the fact that the ancients placed the emphasis on the impulse itself, while we put it on its object. The ancients extolled the impulse and were ready to ennoble through it even an inferior object, while we disparage the activity of the impulse as such and countenance it only because of the merits of the object.

touching and looking, are recognized as preliminary to the sexual aim. These activities are on the one hand themselves connected with pleasure, and on the other hand they enhance the excitement which persists until the definite sexual aim is reached. One definite kind of contiguity, consisting of mutual approximation of the mucuous membranes of the lips in the form of a kiss, has received among the most civilized nations a sexual value, though the parts of the body concerned do not belong to the sexual apparatus but form the entrance to the digestive tract. This therefore supplies the factors which allow us to bring the perversions into relation with the normal sexual life and which are available also for their classification. The perversions are either (*a*) anatomical *transgressions* of the bodily regions destined for sexual union, or (*b*) a *lingering* at the intermediary relations to the sexual object which should normally be rapidly passed on the way to the definite sexual aim.

A. Anatomical Transgression

OVERESTIMATION OF THE SEXUAL OBJECT. The psychic estimation in which the sexual object as a goal of the sexual impulse shares is only in the rarest cases limited to the genitals; generally it embraces the whole body and tends to include all sensations emanating from the sexual object. The same overestimation spreads over the psychic sphere and manifests itself as a logical [24] blinding (diminished judgment) in the face of the psychic attainments and perfections of the sexual object, as well as a blind obedience to the judgments issuing from the latter. The full faith of love thus becomes an important, if not the primordial, source of authority.[14]

It is this sexual overvaluation, which so ill agrees with the

[14] I must mention here that the blind obedience evinced by the hypnotized subject to the hypnotist causes me to think that the nature of hypnosis is to be found in the unconscious fixation of the libido on the person of the hypnotizer (by means of the masochistic component of the sexual impulse). Ferenczi has connected this character of suggestibility with the "parent complex" (*Jahrbuch für psychoanalytische und psychopathologische Forschungen*, I, 1909).

restriction of the sexual aim to the union of the genitals only, that assists other parts of the body to participate as sexual aims.[15]

The significance of the factor of sexual overestimation can be best studied in the man, in whom alone the sexual life is accessible to investigation, whereas in the woman it is veiled in impenetrable darkness, partly in consequence of cultural stunting and partly on account of the conventional reticence and insincerity of women.[16]

SEXUAL UTILIZATION OF THE MUCOUS MEMBRANE OF THE LIPS AND MOUTH. The employment of the mouth as a sexual organ is considered as a perversion if the lips (tongue) of the one are brought into contact with the genitals of the other, but not when the mucous membrane of the lips of both touch each other. In the latter exception we find the connection with the normal. He who abhors the former as perversions, though since antiquity these have been common practices among mankind, yields to a distinct *feeling of loathing* which protects him from adopting such sexual aims. [25] The limit of such loathing is frequently purely conventional; he who kisses fervently the lips of a pretty girl will perhaps be able to use her toothbrush only with a sense of loathing, though there is no reason to assume that his own oral cavity, for which he entertains no loathing, is cleaner than that of the girl. Our attention is here called to the factor of loathing which stands in the way of the libidinous overestimation of the sexual aim but which may in turn be vanquished by the libido. In the loathing we may observe one of the forces which have brought about the restrictions of the sexual aim. As a rule these forces halt at the genitals; there is, however,

[15] At the same time it is to be observed that sexual overestimation is not accomplished by all of the mechanisms of object choice and that later we shall learn of another and direct explanation of the sexual role of other bodily parts. The factor of "excitement hunger" which Hoche and I. Bloch have offered as explanation of the spreading of the sexual interests to parts of the body other than the genitals does not seem to me to serve this significance. The different paths along which the libido moves are related one to another from the phenomenon of collateral streaming.

[16] In typical cases the female permits this sexual overvaluation of the male to pass by but almost never neglects it so far as a child born to her is concerned.

no doubt that even the genitals of the other sex themselves may be an object of loathing. Such behavior is characteristic of all hysterics, especially women. The force of the sexual impulse prefers to occupy itself with the overcoming of this loathing (see later).

Sexual Utilization of the Anal Opening. It is even more obvious than in the former case that it is the loathing which stamps as a perversion the use of the anus as a sexual aim. But it should not be interpreted as espousing a cause when I observe that the basis of this loathing—namely, that this part of the body serves for the excretion and comes in contact with the loathsome excrement—is not more plausible than the basis which hysterical girls have for the disgust which they entertain for the male genital because it serves for urination.

The sexual role of the mucous membrane of the anus is by no means limited to intercourse between men; its preference has nothing characteristic of the inverted feeling. On the contrary, it seems that the *pedicatio* of the man owes its role to the analogy with the act in the woman, whereas among inverts it is mutual masturbation which is the most common sexual aim. [26]

The Significance of Other Parts of the Body. Sexual infringement on the other parts of the body, in all its variations, offers nothing new; it adds nothing to our knowledge of the sexual impulse which herein announces only its intention to dominate the sexual object in every way. Besides the sexual overvaluation, a second and generally unknown factor may be mentioned among the anatomical transgressions. Certain parts of the body, like the mucous membrane of the mouth and anus, which repeatedly appear in such practices, lay claim as it were to be considered and treated as genitals. We shall hear how this claim is justified by the development of the sexual impulse, and how it is fulfilled in the symptomatology of certain morbid conditions.

Unfit Substitutes for the Sexual Object. Fetishism. We are especially impressed by those cases in which for the normal sexual object another is substituted which is related to it but which is totally unfit for the normal sexual aim. According to the scheme of the introduction we should have done better to mention this most interesting group of aberrations of the sexual impulse among the deviations in reference to the sexual object, but we have deferred mention of these until we became acquainted with the factor of sexual overestimation, upon which these manifestations, connected with the relinquishing of the sexual aim, depend.

The substitute for the sexual object is generally a part of the body but little adapted for sexual purposes, such as the foot, or hair, or an inanimate object which is in demonstrable relation with the sexual person, and preferably with the sexuality of the same (fragments of clothing, white underwear). This substitute is not unjustly compared with the fetish in which the savage sees the embodiment of his god.

The transition to the cases of fetishism, with a renunciation of a normal or of a perverted sexual aim, is formed by cases in which a fetishistic determination is demanded in the sexual object [27] if the sexual aim is to be attained (definite color of hair, clothing, even physical blemishes). No other variation of the sexual impulse verging on the pathological claims our interest as much as this one, owing to the peculiarity occasioned by its manifestations. A certain diminution in the striving for the normal sexual aim may be presupposed in all these cases (executive weakness of the sexual apparatus).[17] The connection with the normal is occasioned by the psychologically necessary overestimation of the sexual object, which inevitably encroaches upon everything associatively related to it (sexual object). A certain degree of such fetishism therefore regularly belongs to the normal, especially during those stages of wooing when the normal sexual aim seems inaccessible or its realization deferred:

> "Get me a handkerchief from her bosom—
> a garter of my love." —FAUST

The case becomes pathological only when the striving for the fetish fixes itself beyond such determinations and takes the

[17] This weakness corresponds to the constitutional predisposition. The early sexual intimidation which pushes the person away from the normal sexual aim and urges him to seek a substitute has been demonstrated by psychoanalysis as an accidental determinant.

place of the normal sexual aim; or again, when the fetish disengages itself from the person concerned and itself becomes a sexual object. These are the general determinations for the transition of mere variations of the sexual impulse into pathological aberrations.

The persistent influence of a sexual impression mostly received in early childhood often shows itself in the selection of a fetish, as Binet first asserted, and as was later proved by many illustrations—a thing which may be placed parallel to the proverbial attachment to a first love in the normal (*"On revient tojours à ses premiers amours"*). [28] Such a connection is especially seen in cases with only fetishistic determinations of the sexual object. The significance of early sexual impressions will be met again in other places.[18]

In other cases it was mostly a symbolic thought association, unconscious to the person concerned, which led to the replacing of the object by means of a fetish. The paths of these connections can not always be definitely demonstrated. The foot is a very primitive sexual symbol already found in myths.[19] Fur is used as a fetish probably on account of its association with the hairiness of the mons veneris. Such symbolism seems often to depend on sexual experiences in childhood.[20] [29]

[18] Deeper penetrating psychoanalytic investigation has led to a more authoritative critique of Binet's assertion. All observations dealing with this subject show that there is a first encounter with the fetish wherein it already shows itself to be in possession of the sexual interest. From the accompanying circumstances one cannot, however, understand how it came into possession of this interest. Moreover, all these "early" sexual impressions occur after the fifth to sixth year, whereas psychoanalysis permits itself to doubt whether such pathological fixations can take place as new formations at so late a date. The actual facts are that behind the first memories concerning the appearance of the fetish there lies a submerged and forgottén phase of the sexual development for which the fetish acts as a substitute or conceals a "cover memory" and also represented the residue as well as the precipitate of this sexual phase. The changing the phase of fetishism which takes place during the first years of childhood, as well as the choice of the fetish itself, is constitutionally determined.

[19] The shoe or slipper is accordingly a symbol for the female genitals.

[20] Psychoanalysis has filled up the gap in the understanding of fetishisms by showing that the selection of the fetish depends on a

B. Fixation of Precursory Sexual Aims

THE APPEARANCE OF NEW INTENTIONS. All the outer and inner determinations which impede or hold at a distance the attainment of the normal sexual aim, such as impotence, costliness of the sexual object, and dangers of the sexual act, will conceivably strengthen the inclination to linger at the preparatory acts and to form them into new sexual aims which may take the place of the normal. On closer investigation it is always seen that the ostensibly most peculiar of these new intentions have already been indicated in the normal sexual act.

TOUCHING AND LOOKING. At least a certain amount of touching is indispensable for a person in order to attain the normal sexual aim. It is also generally known that the touching of the skin of the sexual object causes much pleasure and produces a supply of new excitement. Hence, the lingering at the touching can hardly be considered a perversion if the sexual act is proceeded with.

The same holds true in the end with looking, which is analogous to touching. The manner in which the libidinous excitement is frequently awakened is by the optical impressions, and selection takes account of this circumstance—if this teleogical mode of thinking be permitted—by making the sexual object a thing of beauty. The covering of the body, which keeps abreast with civilization, serves to arouse sexual inquisitiveness, which always strives to restore for itself the sexual object by uncovering the hidden parts. This can be turned

---

coprophilic smell-desire which has been lost by repression. Feet and hair are strong-smelling objects which are raised to fetishes after the renouncing of the now unpleasant sensation of smell. Accordingly, only the filthy and ill-smelling foot is the sexual object in the perversion which corresponds to the foot fetishism. Another contribution to the explanation of the fetishistic preference of the foot is found in the Infantile Séxual Theories (see later). The foot replaces the penis which is so much missed in the woman. In some cases of foot fetishism it could be shown that the deire for looking originally directed to the genitals, which wished to reach its object from below, was stopped on the way by prohibition and repression, and therefore adhered to the foot or shoe as a fetish. In conformity with infantile expectation, the female genital was hereby imagined as a male genital.

into the artistic ("sublimation") if the interest is turned from the genitals to the form of the body.[21] The tendency to linger at this intermediary sexual [30] aim of the sexually accentuated looking is found to a certain degree in most normals; indeed it gives them the possibility of directing a certain amount of their libido to a higher artistic aim. On the other hand, the fondness for looking becomes a perversion (*a*) when it limits itself entirely to the genitals; (*b*) when it becomes connected with the overcoming of loathing (voyeurs and onlookers at the functions of excretion); and (*c*) when instead of preparing for the normal sexual aim it suppresses it. The latter, if I may draw conclusions from a single analysis, is in a most pronounced way true of exhibitionists, who expose their genitals so as in turn to bring to view the genitals of others.[22]

In the perversion which consists in striving to look and be looked at we are confronted with a very remarkable character which will occupy us even more intensively in the following aberration. The sexual aim is here present in twofold formation, in an *active* and a *passive* form.

The force which is opposed to the peeping mania and through which it is eventually abolished is *shame* (like the former *loathing*).

SADISM AND MASOCHISM. The tendency to cause pain to the sexual object and its opposite, the most frequent and most significant of all perversions, was designated in its two forms by v. Krafft-Ebing as sadism for the active form, and masochism for the passive form. Other authors prefer the narrower term algolagnia, which emphasizes the pleasure in pain and cruelty, whereas the terms selected by v. Krafft-Ebing

[21] I have no doubt that the conception of the "beautiful" is rooted in the soil of sexual stimulation and signified originally that which is sexually exciting. The more remarkable, therefore, is the fact that the genitals, the sight of which provokes the greatest sexual excitement, can really never be considered "beautiful."

[22] Analysis reveals this perversion—just as most others—to have an unexpected multiplicity of motivations and meanings. Exhibitionism, for instance, is strongly dependent upon the castration complex; it would emphasize again the integrity of one's own (male) genitals and repeats the infantile satisfaction of the lack of the penis in the female.

place the pleasure secured in all kinds of humility and submission in the foreground. [31]

The roots of active algolagnia, sadism, can be readily demonstrable in the normal individual. The sexuality of most men shows an admixture of *aggression*, of a propensity to subdue, the biological significance of which lies in the necessity for overcoming the resistance of the sexual object by actions other than mere *courting*. Sadism would then correspond to an aggressive component of the sexual impulse which has become independent and exaggerated and has been brought to the foreground by displacement.

The conception of sadism fluctuates in everyday speech from a mere active or impetuous attitude toward the sexual object to the exclusive attachment of the gratification to the subjection and maltreatment of the object. Strictly speaking, only the last extreme case has a claim to the name of perversion.

Similarly, the designation masochism comprises all passive attitudes to the sexual life and to the sexual object; in its most extreme form the gratification is connected with suffering of physical or mental pain at the hands of the sexual object. Masochism as a perversion seems further removed from the normal sexual goal than its opposite. It may even be doubted whether it ever is primary; much oftener, it probably arises through transformation from sadism.[23] It can often be recognized that masochism is nothing but a continuation of sadism directed against one's own person in which the latter at first takes the place of the sexual object. [32] Clinical analysis of extreme cases of masochistic perversions show that there is a cooperation of a large series of factors which exaggerate and

[23] Later reflections which can be supported by definite evidence concerning the structure of the mental systems and of the activities of instincts therein have changed my judgment concerning masochism very widely. I have been led to recognize a primary erotogenic masochism from which there develop two later forms, a feminine and a moral masochism. Through a turning back of an unconsumed sadism directed against oneself during life there arises a secondary masochism which becomes added to the primary masochism. (See Freud, "Das ökonomische Problem des Masochismus," *Int. Zeit. f. Psa.*, X, 121, 1924. Translated into English in Hogarth Press *Collected Papers,* Vol. II, p. 255.)

fix the original passive sexual attitude (castration complex, conscience).

The pain which is here overcome ranks with the loathing and shame which were the resistances opposed to the libido.

Sadism and masochism occupy a special place among the perversions, for the contrast of activity and passivity lying at their bases belong to the common traits of the sexual life.

That cruelty and sexual impulse are most intimately connected is beyond doubt taught by the history of civilization, but in the explanation of this connection no one has gone beyond the accentuation of the aggressive factors of the libido. The aggression which is mixed with the sexual impulse is according to some authors a remnant of cannibalistic lust, a participation on the part of the domination apparatus (*Bemächtigungsapparates*), which served also for the gratification of the great wants of the other, ontogenetically older impulse.[24] It has also been claimed that every pain contains in itself the possibility of a pleasurable sensation. Let us be satisfied with the impression that the explanation of this perversion is by no means satisfactory and that it is possible that many psychic efforts unite themselves into one effect.[25]

The most striking peculiarity of this perversion lies in the fact that its active and passive forms are regularly encountered together in the same person. He who experiences pleasure by causing pain to others in sexual relations is also able to experience the pain emanating from sexual relations as [33] pleasure. A sadist is simultaneously a masochist, though either the active or the passive side of the perversion may be more strongly developed and thus represent his preponderate sexual activity.[26]

We thus see that certain perverted propensities regularly appear in *contrasting pairs,* a thing which, in view of the

[24] Cf. here the later studies on the pregenital phases of the sexual development, in which this view is confirmed.

[25] From the researches just cited.

[26] Instead of substantiating this statement by many examples, I shall merely cite Havelock Ellis (*The Sexual Impulse,* 1903): "All known cases of sadism and masochism, even those cited by v. Krafft-Ebing, always show (as has already been shown by Colin, Scott, and Féré) traces of both groups of manifestations in the same individual."

material to be produced later, must claim great theoretical value.[27] It is furthermore clear that the existence of the contrast, sadism and masochism, can not readily be attributed to the mixture of aggression. On the other hand one may be tempted to connect such simultaneously existing contrasts with the united contrast of male and female in bisexuality, the significance of which is reduced in psychoanalysis to the contrast of activity and passivity.

3. GENERAL STATEMENTS APPLICABLE TO ALL PERVERSIONS

VARIATION AND DISEASE. The physicians who at first studied the *perversions* in pronounced cases and under peculiar conditions were naturally inclined to attribute to them the character of a morbid or degenerative sign similar to the *inversions*. This view, however, is easier to refute in this than in the former case. Everyday experience has shown that most of these transgressions, at least the milder ones, are seldom wanting as components in the sexual life of normals who look upon them as upon other intimacies. Wherever the conditions are favorable such a perversion may for a long time be substituted by a [34] normal person for the normal sexual aim or it may be placed near it. In no normal person does the normal sexual aim lack some designable perverse element, and this universality suffices in itself to prove the inexpediency of an approbrious application of the name perversion. In the realm of the sexual life one is sure to meet with exceptional difficulties, which are at present really unsolvable, if one wishes to draw a sharp line between the mere variations within physiological limits and morbid symptoms.

Nevertheless, the quality of the new sexual aim in some of these perversions is such as to require special notice. Some of the perversions are in content so distant from the normal that we cannot help calling them "morbid," especially those in which the sexual impulse, in overcoming the resistances (shame, loathing, fear, and pain) has brought about surprising results (licking of feces and violation of cadavers). Yet

[27] See later discussion of "Ambivalence."

even in these cases one ought not to feel certain of regularly finding among the perpetrators persons of pronounced abnormalities or insane minds. We can not lose sight of the fact that persons who otherwise behave normally are recorded as sick in the realm of the sexual life where they are dominated by the most unbridled of all impulses. On the other hand, a manifest abnormality in any other relation in life generally shows an undercurrent of abnormal sexual behavior.

In the majority of cases we are able to find the morbid character of the perversion not in the content of the new sexual aim but in its relation to the normal. It is morbid if the perversion does not appear beside the normal (sexual aim and sexual object), where favorable circumstances promote it and unfavorable [35] impede the normal, or if it has under all circumstances repressed and supplanted the normal; *the exclusiveness* and *fixation* of the perversion justify us in considering it a morbid symptom.

THE PSYCHIC PARTICIPATION IN THE PERVERSIONS. Perhaps it is precisely in the most abominable perversions that we must recognize the most prolific psychic participation for the transformation of the sexual impulse. In these cases a piece of psychic work has been accomplished in which, in spite of its gruesome success, the value of an idealization of the impulse can not be disputed. The omnipotence of love nowhere perhaps shows itself stronger than in this one of her aberrations. The highest and the lowest everywhere in sexuality hang most intimately together. ("From heaven through the world to hell.")

TWO RESULTS. In the study of perversions we have gained an insight into the fact that the sexual impulse has to struggle against certain psychic forces, resistances, among which shame and loathing are most prominent. We may presume that these forces are employed to confine the impulse within the accepted normal limits, and if they have become developed in the individual before the sexual impulse has attained its full strength, it is really they which have directed it in the course of development.[28]

[28] On the other hand the restricting forces of sexual evolution—disgust, shame, morality—must also be looked upon as historical

We have furthermore remarked that some of the examined perversions can be comprehended only by assuming the union of many motives. If they are amenable to analysis—disintegration—they must be of a composite nature. This may give us a hint that the sexual impulse itself may not be something simple, that [36] it may on the contrary be composed of many components which detach themselves to form perversions. Our clinical observation thus calls our attention to *fusions* which have lost their expression in the uniform normal behavior.[29]

4. THE SEXUAL IMPULSE IN NEUROTICS

PSYCHOANALYSIS. A proper contribution to the knowledge of the sexual impulse in persons who are at least related to the normal can be gained only from one source, and is accessible only by one definite path. There is only one way to obtain a thorough and unerring solution of problems in the sexual life of so-called psychoneurotics (hysteria, obsessions, the wrongly named neurasthenia, and surely also dementia præcox and paranoia), and that is by subjecting them to the psychoanalytic investigations propounded by J. Breuer and myself in 1893, which we called the "cathartic" treatment.

I must repeat what I have said in other publications, that these psychoneuroses, as far as my experience goes, are based on sexual-instinct motive powers. I do not mean that the energy of the sexual impulse merely contributes to the forces supporting the morbid manifestations (symptoms), but I wish distinctly to maintain that this supplies the only constant and

---

precipitates of the outer inhibitions which the sexual impulse experienced in the psychogenesis of humanity. One can observe that they appear in their time during the development of the individual as if spontaneously at the call of education and influence.

[29] I would make the anticipatory comment concerning the origin of the perversions that there is present a disposition to normal sexual development before their fixation, exactly as in the case of fetishism. Analytical study has thus far been able to show in individual cases that the perversion is an arrest in the development of the Œdipus complex, following which repression, according to their anlage, the strongest components of the sexual instinct appear.

the most important source of energy in the neurosis, so that the sexual life of such persons manifests itself either exclusively, preponderately, or partially in [37] these symptoms. As I have already stated in different places, the symptoms are the sexual activities of the patient. The proof for this assertion I have obtained from an increasing number of hysterics and other neurotics during a period of twenty-five years, the results of which in individual cases I have already given in detail in other communications and still hope to report.[30]

Psychoanalysis allays the symptoms of hysteria on the supposition that they are the substitutes—the transcriptions as it were—for a series of emotionally accentuated psychic processes, wishes, and desires, to which a passage for their discharge through the conscious psychic activities has been cut off by a special process (repression). These thought formations which are restricted in the state of the unconscious strive for expression, that is, for *discharge*, in conformity to their affective value, and find such in hysteria through a process of *conversion* into somatic phenomena—the hysterical symptom. If, *lege artis*, and with the aid of a special technique, retrogressive transformations of the symptoms into the affectful and conscious thoughts can be effected, it then becomes possible to get the most accurate information about the nature and origin of these previously unconscious psychic formations.

RESULTS OF PSYCHOANALYSIS. In this manner it has been discovered that the symptoms represent the equivalent for the strivings which received their strength from the source of the sexual impulse. This fully concurs with what we know of the character of hysterics, which we have taken as models for all psychoneurotics, before they have become diseased, and [38] with what we know concerning the causes of the disease. The hysterical character evinces a part of sexual repression which reaches beyond the normal limits, an exaggeration of the resistances against the sexual impulse which we know as shame and loathing. It is an instinctive flight from intellectual oc-

[30] It is a more complete statement, rather than a diminution of it, when I would modify it thus: Nervous symptoms depend on the one hand upon the claims of the libidinous impulses, on the other upon the protest of the Ego and its reactions against the same.

cupation with the sexual problem, the consequence of which in pronounced cases is a complete sexual ignorance, which is preserved till the age of sexual maturity is attained.[31]

This feature, so characteristic of hysteria, is not seldom concealed in crude observation by the existence of the second constitutional factor of hysteria, namely, the enormous development of the sexual craving. But the psychological analysis will always reveal it, and solves the very contradictory enigma of hysteria by proving the existence of the contrasting pair, an immense sexual desire and a very exaggerated sexual rejection.

The provocation of the disease in hysterically predisposed persons is brought about if in consequence of their progressive maturity or external conditions of life they are earnestly confronted with the real sexual demand. Between the pressure of the craving and the opposition of the sexual rejection an outlet for the disease results, which does not remove the conflict but seeks to elude it by transforming the libidinous strivings into symptoms. It is an exception only in appearance if a hysterical person, say a man, becomes subject to some banal emotional disturbance, to a conflict in the center of which there is no sexual interest. Psychoanalysis will regularly show that it is the sexual [39] components of the conflict which make the disease possible by withdrawing the psychic processes from normal adjustment.

NEUROSIS AND PERVERSION. A great part of the opposition to this assertion of mine is explained by the fact that the sexuality from which I deduce the psychoneurotic symptoms is thought of as coincident with the normal sexual impulse. But psychoanalysis teaches us better than this. It shows that the symptoms do not by any means result at the expense only of the so-called normal sexual impulse (at least not exclusively or preponderately), but they represent the converted expression of impulses which in a broader sense might be designated as *perverse* if they could manifest themselves directly in fantasies

[31] *Studien über Hysterie*, 1895 (in English in Nervous and Mental Disease Monograph Series, No. 4). J. Breuer tells of the patient with whom he first practiced the cathartic method: "The sexual factor was surprisingly undeveloped."

and acts without deviating from consciousness. The symptoms are therefore partially formed at the cost of abnormal sexuality. *The neurosis is, so to say, the negative of the perversion.*[32]

The sexual impulse of the psychoneurotic shows all the aberrations which we have studied as variations of the normal and as manifestations of morbid sexual life.

(*a*) In all neurotics we find without exception in the unconscious psychic life feelings of inversion and fixation of libido on persons of the same sex. Without a deep and searching discussion it is impossible adequately to appreciate the significance of this factor for the formation of the picture of the disease; I can only assert that the *unconscious* propensity to inversion is never wanting and is particularly of immense service in explaining male hysteria.[33] [40]

(*b*) All the inclinations to anatomical transgression can be demonstrated in psychoneurotics in the unconscious and as symptom creators. Of special frequency and intensity are those which impart to the mouth and the mucous membrane of the anus the role of genitals.

(*c*) The partial desires which usually appear in contrasting pairs play a very prominent role among the symptom creators in the psychoneuroses. We have learned to know them as carriers of new sexual aims, such as peeping mania, exhibitionism, and the actively and passively formed impulses of cruelty. The contribution of the last is indispensable for the understanding of the morbid nature of the symptoms; it almost regularly controls some portion of the social behavior of the patient. The transformation of love into hatred, of tenderness into hostility, which is characteristic of a large number

[32] The well known fancies of perverts which under favorable conditions are changed into contrivances, the delusional fears of paranoiacs which are in a hostile manner projected on others, and the unconscious fancies of hysterics which are discovered in their symptoms by psychoanalysis, agree as to content in the minutest details.

[33] A psychoneurosis very often associates itself with a manifest inversion in which the heterosexual feeling becomes subjected to complete repression. It is but just to state that the necessity of a general recognition of the tendency to inversion in psychoneurotics was first imparted to me personally by Wilh. Fliess, of Berlin, after I had myself discovered it in some cases. This fact, not sufficiently valued, must markedly influence all theories of homosexuality.

of neurotic cases and apparently of all cases of paranoia, takes place by means of the union of cruelty with the libido.

The interest in these deductions will be more heightened by certain peculiarities of the actual facts.

1. Wherever any such impulse is found in the unconscious which can be paired with a contrasting one, it can regularly be demonstrated that the latter, too, is effective. Every active perversion is here accompanied by its passive counterpart. He who in the unconscious is an exhibitionist is at the same time a voyeur; he who suffers from sadistic feelings as a result of repression will also show another reinforcement of the symptoms from the source of masochistic tendencies. The perfect concurrence with the behavior of the corresponding positive perversions is certainly very noteworthy. [41] In the picture of the disease, however, the preponderant role is played by either one or the other of the opposing tendencies.

2. In a pronounced case of psychoneurosis we seldom find the development of a single perverted impulse; usually there are many, and regularly there are traces of all perversions. The individual impulse, however, because of its intensity, is independent of the development of the others, but the study of the positive perversions gives us the accurate counterpart to it.

5. PARTIAL IMPULSES AND EROGENOUS ZONES

Keeping in mind what we have learned from the examination of the positive and negative perversions, it becomes quite obvious that they can be referred to as a number of "partial impulses," which are not, however, primary but are subject to further analysis. By an "instinct" we can understand in the first place nothing but the psychic representative of a continually flowing inner somatic source of stimulation to be distinguished from "stimulus" which comes from combined external excitations. "Instinct" is thus one of the concepts marking the limits between the psychic and the physical. The simplest and most obvious assumption concerning the nature of instincts would be that in themselves they possess no quality but are taken into account only as a measure of the demand for effort in the psychic life. What distinguishes the impulses from one another and furnishes them with specific attributes is their relation to their somatic *sources* and to their *aims.* The source of the impulse is an exciting process in an organ, and the immediate aim of the [42] impulse lies in the release of this organ stimulus.[34]

A further provisional assumption in the theory of the instincts which we cannot relinquish states that from the bodily organs two kinds of excitation arise which are founded upon differences of a chemical nature. One of these forms of overstimulation can be designated as the specifically sexual and the concerned organ as the *erogenous zone,* while the sexual element emanating from it is the partial impulse.[35]

In the perversions which claim sexual significance for the oral cavity and the anal opening, the part played by the erogenous zone is quite obvious. These tendencies behave in every way like a part of the sexual apparatus. In hysteria these parts of the body, as well as the tracts of mucous membrane proceeding from them, become the seat of new sensations and innervating changes in a manner similar to the real genitals when under the excitement of normal sexual processes.

In the psychoneuroses the significance of the erogenous zones as additional apparatus and substitutes for the genitals appears to be most prominent in hysteria, though that does not signify that it is of lesser validity in the other morbid forms. It is not so recognizable in compulsion neurosis and paranoia because here the symptom formation takes place in regions of the psychic apparatus which lie at a great distance

[34] The science of the instincts is the most significant but the most incomplete part of the psychoanalytic theory. In my later works (*Jenseits des Lustprinzips* [*Beyond the Pleasure Principle*], English by Boni & Liveright, N.Y., and *Das Ich und Das Es,* 1925 [*The Ego and the Id*], English Internat. Psychoanalytic Press, London) I have developed further contributions to the study of the instincts.

[35] It is not easy to justify here these assumptions which are taken from a definite class of neurotic diseases. On the other hand, it would be impossible to assert anything definite concerning the instincts if one did not take the trouble of mentioning these presuppositions.

from the central locations for bodily control. The more remarkable thing in the compulsion neurosis is the significance of the impulses which create new sexual aims and appear independently of the erogenous zones. [43] Nevertheless, the eye corresponds to an erogenous zone in the looking and exhibition mania, while the skin takes on the same part in the pain and cruelty components of the sexual impulse. The skin, which in special parts of the body becomes differentiated as sensory organs and modified by the mucous membrane, is the erogenous zone, κατ ἐξοχήν.[36]

6. EXPLANATION OF THE SEEMING PREPONDERANCE OF SEXUAL PERVERSIONS IN THE PSYCHONEUROSES

The sexuality of psychoneurotics has perhaps been placed in a false light by the above discussions. It appears that the sexual behavior of the psychoneurotic approaches in predisposition to the pervert and deviates by just so much from the normal. Nevertheless, it is very possible that the constitutional disposition of these patients, besides containing an immense amount of sexual repression and a predominant force of sexual impulse, also possesses an unusual tendency to perversions in the broadest sense. However, an examination of milder cases shows that the last assumption is not an absolute requisite, or at least that in pronouncing judgment on the morbid effects one ought to discount the effect of one of the factors. In most psychoneurotics the disease first appears after puberty, following the demands of the normal sexual life. Against these the repression above all directs itself. Or the disease comes on later, owing to the fact that the libido is unable to attain normal sexual gratification. In both cases the libido behaves like a stream the principal bed of which is dammed; it fills the collateral roads which until now perhaps [44] have been empty. Thus the manifestly great (though to be sure negative) tendency to perversion in psychoneurotics

[36] One should here think of Moll's assertion, who divides the sexual instinct into the impulses of contrectation and detumescence. Contrectation signifies a desire to touch the skin.

may be collaterally conditioned; at any rate, it is certainly collaterally increased. The fact of the matter is that the sexual repression has to be added as an inner factor to such external ones as restriction of freedom, inaccessibility to the normal sexual object, dangers of the normal sexual act, and so on, which cause the origin of perversions in individuals who might have otherwise remained normal.

In individual cases of neurosis the behavior may be different; now the congenital force of the tendency to perversion may be more decisive, and at other times more influence may be exerted by the collateral increase of the same through the deviation of the libido from the normal sexual aim and object. It would be unjust to construe a contrast where a cooperation exists. The greatest results will always be brought about by a neurosis if constitution and experience cooperate in the same direction. A pronounced constitution may perhaps be able to dispense with the assistance of daily impressions, while a profound disturbance in life may perhaps bring on a neurosis even in an average constitution. These views similarly hold true in the etiological significance of the congenital and the accidental experiences in other spheres.

If, however, preference is given to the assumption that an especially formed tendency to perversions is characteristic of the psychoneurotic constitution, there is a prospect of being able to distinguish a multiformity of such constitutions in accordance with the congenital preponderance of this or that erogenous zone, or of this or that partial impulse. Whether there is a special relationship between the predisposition to perversions and the selection of the morbid picture has not, like many other things in this realm, been investigated. [45]

7. REFERENCE TO THE INFANTILISM OF SEXUALITY

By demonstrating the perverted feelings as symptom formations in psychoneurotics, we have enormously increased the number of persons who can be added to the perverts. This is not only because neurotics represent a very large proportion of humanity; we must consider also that the neuroses in all their gradations run in an uninterrupted series to the normal state. Moebius was quite justified in saying that we are all somewhat hysterical. Hence, the very wide dissemination of perversions urged us to assume that the predisposition to perversions is no rare peculiarity but must form a part of the normally accepted constitution.

We have heard that it is a question whether perversions should be referred to congenital determinations or whether they originate from accidental experiences, just as Binet showed in fetishisms. Now we are forced to the conclusion that there is indeed something congenital at the basis of perversions, but it is something *which is congenital in all persons,* which as a predisposition may fluctuate in intensity and is brought into prominence by influences of life. We deal here with congenital roots in the constitution of the sexual impulse which in one series of cases develop into real carriers of sexual activity (perverts); while in other cases they undergo an insufficient suppression (repression), so that as morbid symptoms they are enabled to attract to themselves in a roundabout way a considerable part of the sexual energy; while again in favorable cases between the two extremes they originate the normal sexual life through effective restrictions and other elaborations.

But we must also remember that the assumed constitution which shows the roots of all perversions will be demonstrable [46] only in the child, though all impulses can be manifested in it only in moderate intensity. If we are led to suppose that neurotics conserve the infantile state of their sexuality or return to it, our interest must then turn to the sexual life of the child, and we shall then follow the play of influences which control the processes of development of the infantile sexuality up to its termination in a perversion, a neurosis or a normal sexual life. [47]

Contribution II

INFANTILE SEXUALITY

THE NEGLECT OF THE INFANTILE. It is a part of popular belief about the sexual impulse that it is absent in childhood and that it first appears in the period of life known as puberty. This, though a common error, is serious in its consequences and is chiefly due to our present ignorance of the fundamental principles of the sexual life. A comprehensive study of the sexual manifestations of childhood would probably reveal to us the existence of the essential features of the sexual impulse, and would make us acquainted with its development and its composition from various sources.

It is remarkable that those writers who endeavor to explain the qualities and reactions of the adult individual have given so much more attention to the ancestral period than to the period of the individual's own existence—that is, they have attributed more influence to heredity than to childhood. As a matter of fact, it might well be supposed that the influence of the latter period would be easier to understand and that it would be entitled to more consideration than heredity.[1] To be sure, one occasionally finds in medical literature [48] notes on the premature sexual activities of small children, about erections and masturbation and even actions resembling coitus, but these are referred to merely as exceptional occurrences, as curiosities, or as deterring examples of premature perversity. No author has to my knowledge recognized the normality of the sexual impulse in childhood, and in the numerous writings on the development of the child the chapter on "Sexual Development" is usually passed over.[2]

[1] For it is really impossible to have a correct knowledge of the part belonging to heredity without first understanding the part belonging to the infantile.

[2] On revision this assertion seemed even to myself so bold that I decided to test its correctness by again reviewing the literature. The result of this second review did not warrant any change in

INFANTILE AMNESIA. The ground for this remarkable negligence I seek partly [49] in conventional considerations, which influence writers on account of their own bringing up, and partly to a psychic phenomenon which thus far has remained unexplained. I refer to the peculiar amnesia which veils from most people (not from all) the first years of their childhood, usually the first six or eight years. So far it has not occurred to us that this amnesia ought to surprise us, though we have good reasons for surprise. For we are informed that in those years from which we later obtain nothing except a

---

my original statement. The scientific elaboration of the physical as well as the psychic phenomena of the infantile sexuality is still in its initial stages. One author (S. Bell, "A Preliminary Study of the Emotions of Love Between the Sexes," *American Journal of Psychology*, XIII, 1902) says: "I know of no scientist who has given a careful analysis of the emotion as it is seen in the adolescent." The only attention given to somatic sexual manifestations occurring before the age of puberty has been in connection with degenerative manifestations, and these were referred to as a sign of degeneration. A chapter on the sexual life of children is not to be found in all the representative psychologies of this age which I have read. Among these works I can mention the following: Preyer, Baldwin (*The Development of the Mind in the Child and in the Race*, 1898); Pérez (*L'enfant de 3–7 ans*, 1894); Strümpell (*Die pädagogische Pathologie*, 1899); Karl Groos (*Das Seelenleben des Kindes*, 1904); Th. Heller (*Grundriss der Heilpädagogic*, 1904); Sully (*Observations Concerning Childhood*, 1897), and others. The best impression of the present situation of this sphere can be obtained from the journal *Die Kinderfehler* (issued since 1896). On the other hand one gains the impression that the existence of love in childhood is in no need of demonstration. Pérez *(loc. cit.)* speaks for it; K. Groos (*Die Spiele der Menschen*, 1899) states that some children are very early subject to sexual emotions, and show a desire to touch the other sex (p. 336); S. Bell observed the earliest appearance of sex-love in a child during the middle part of its third year. See also Havelock Ellis, *The Sexual Impulse*, Appendix II.

The above-mentioned judgment concerning the literature of infantile sexuality no longer holds true since the appearance of the great and important work of G. Stanley Hall (*Adolescence: Its Psychology and Its Relation to Physiology, Anthropology, Sociology, Sex, Crime, Religion, and Education*, 2 vols. [New York, 1908]. The recent book of A. Moll, *Das Sexuelleben des Kindes* (Berlin, 1909), offers no occasion for such a modification. See, on the other hand, Bleuler, "Sexuelle Abnormitäten der Kinder" (*Jahrbuch der schweizerischen Gesellschaft für Schulgesundheitspflege*, IX, 1908). A book by Mrs. Dr. H. v. Hug-Hellmuth, *Aus dem Seelenleben des Kindes*, 1913, has taken full account of the neglected sexual factors. [Translated in Monograph Series, No. 29.]

few incomprehensible memory fragments, we have vividly reacted to impressions, that we have manifested pain and pleasure like any human being, that we have evinced love, jealousy, and other passions as they then affected us; indeed, we are told that we have uttered remarks which proved to grown-ups that we possessed understanding and a budding power of judgment. Still, we know nothing of all this when we become older. Why does our memory lag behind all our other psychic activities? We really have reason to believe that at no time of life are we more capable of impressions and reproductions than during the years of childhood.[3]

On the other hand we must assume, or we may convince ourselves through psychological observations on others, that the very impressions which we have forgotten have nevertheless left the deepest traces in our phychic life, and acted as determinants for our whole future development. We conclude therefore that we [50] do not deal with a real forgetting of infantile impressions but rather with an amnesia similar to that observed in neurotics for later experiences, the nature of which consists in their being detained from consciousness (repression). But what forces bring about this repression of the infantile impressions? He who can solve this riddle will also explain hysterical amnesia.

We shall not, however, hesitate to assert that the existence of the infantile amnesia gives us a new point of comparison between the psychic states of the child and those of the psychoneurotic. We have already encountered another point of comparison when confronted by the fact that the sexuality of the psychoneurotic preserves the infantile character or has returned to it. May there not be an ultimate connection between the infantile and the hysterical amnesias?

The connection between infantile and hysterical amnesias is really more than a mere play of wit. Hysterical amnesia which serves the repression can be explained only by the fact that the individual already possesses a sum of recollections

[3] I have attempted to solve the problems presented by the earliest infantile recollections in a paper, "Ueber Deckerinnerungen" (*Monatsschrift für Psychiatrie und Neurologie*, VI, 1899). Cf. also *The Psychopathology of Everyday Life* (The Macmillan Co., New York, and Unwin, London).

which have been withdrawn from conscious disposal and which by associative connection now seize that which is acted upon by the repelling forces of the repression emanating from consciousness.[4] We may say that without infantile amnesia there would be no hysterical amnesia.

I believe that infantile amnesia which causes the individual to look upon his childhood as if it were a *prehistoric* time and conceals from him the beginning of his own sexual life—that this amnesia is responsible for the fact that one does not usually attribute any value to the infantile period in the development of the sexual life. A single observer cannot fill the gap which [51] has been thus produced in our knowledge. As early as 1896 I had already emphasized the significance of childhood for the origin of certain important phenomena connected with the sexual life, and since then I have not ceased to put into the foreground the importance of the infantile factor for sexuality.

THE SEXUAL LATENCY PERIOD OF CHILDHOOD AND ITS INTERRUPTIONS

The extraordinary frequent discoveries of apparently abnormal and exceptional sexual manifestations in childhood, as well as the discovery of infantile reminiscences in neurotics, which were hitherto unconscious, allow us to sketch the following picture of the sexual behavior of childhood.[5]

It seems certain that the newborn child brings with it the germs of sexual feelings which continue to develop for some time and then succumb to a progressive suppression, which is in turn broken through by the proper advances of the sexual development and which can be checked by individual idiosyncrasies. Nothing is known concerning the laws and peri-

[4] One cannot understand the mechanism of repression if one takes into consideration only one of the two cooperating processes. As a comparison one may think of the way the tourist is dispatched to the top of the great pyramid of Gizeh; he is pushed from below and pulled from above.

[5] The use of the latter material is justified by the fact that the years of childhood of those who are later neurotics need not necessarily differ from those who are later normal except in intensity and distinctness.

odicity of this oscillating course of development. It seems, however, that the sexual life of the child mostly manifests itself in the third or fourth year in some form accessible to observation.[6] [52]

SEXUAL INHIBITION. It is during this period of total or at least partial latency that the psychic forces develop which later act as inhibitions on the sexual life, and narrow its direction like dams. These psychic forces are loathing, shame, and moral and esthetic ideal demands. We may gain the impression that the erection of these dams in the civilized child is the work of education; and surely education contributes much to it. In reality, however, this development is organically determined and can occasionally be produced without the

[6] An anatomic analogy to the behavior of the infantile sexual function formulated by me is perhaps given by Bayer (*Deutsches Archiv für klinische Medizin*, Bd. 73) who claims that the internal genitals (uterus) are regularly larger in newborn than in older children. However, Halban's conception, that after birth there is also an involution of the other parts of the sexual apparatus, has not been verified. According to Halban (*Zeitschrift für Geburtshilfe u. Gynäkologie*, LIII, 1904) this process of involution ends after a few weeks of extrauterine life. The authors who regard the interstitial portions of the sex glands as the sex-determining organs have been led through their anatomical study to discuss for their part infantile sexuality and the sexual latency periods.

I cite from page 20 of Lipschütz's book on the puberty glands. One would more correctly represent the facts by saying that the maturing of the sexual characteristics as seen fully in puberty depends upon the increased rapid development of processes which have begun much earlier—according to our opinion even in embryonal life. "What one heretofore has designated—and badly—as puberty, is probably only a second great phase of puberty which sets in in the middle of the second decade in life.—Childhood reckoned from birth to the second great phase we can thus designate as an intermediary phase of puberty."—In a report of Ferenczi (*Int. Zeit. f. Psa.*, VI, 1920) this general correspondence between anatomical finding and psychological observation is disturbed by the one statement that the first apex of development of the sexual organs takes place in the earliest embryonal time, whereas the early blossoming of the sexual life of the child is to be found in the third and fourth year. The complete synchronization of anatomical preparation and psychical development is naturally not necessary. The pertinent investigations have still to be made upon the gonads of humans. Since in animals there is no latent period, psychologically considered, much is still to be learned whether the anatomical findings upon which foundations the authors assume two points of apical growth in the sexual development can be demonstrated also on other higher animals.

help of education. Indeed education remains properly within its assigned realm only if it strictly follows the path of the organic determinant and impresses it somewhat cleaner and deeper.

REACTION FORMATION AND SUBLIMATION. What are the means that accomplish these very important constructions so significant for the later personal culture and normality? They are probably brought about at the cost of the infantile sexuality itself [53] the influx of which has not stopped even in this latency period–the energy of which indeed has been turned away either wholly or partially from sexual utilization and conducted to other aims. The historians of civilization seem to be unanimous in the opinion that such deviation of sexual motive powers from sexual aims to new aims, a process which merits the name of *sublimation*, has furnished powerful components for all cultural accomplishments. We shall therefore add that the same process acts in the development of every individual and that it begins to act in the sexual latency period.[7]

We can also venture an opinion about the mechanisms of such sublimation. The sexual feelings of these infantile years on the one hand could not be utilizable, since the procreating functions are postponed—this is the chief character of the latency period; on the other hand, they would in themselves be perverse, as they would emanate from erogenous zones and would be born of impulses which in the individual's course of development could only evoke a feeling of displeasure. They therefore awaken contrary forces (feelings of reaction), which displeasure builds up the already mentioned psychical dams such as disgust, shame and morality.[8]

THE INTERRUPTIONS OF THE LATENCY PERIOD. Without deluding ourselves as to the hypothetical nature and deficient clearness of our understanding regarding the infantile period

[7] The expression "sexual latency period" *(sexuelle latenz-periode)* I have borrowed from W. Fliess.

[8] In the case here discussed, sublimation of the sexual motive powers proceeds on the road of reaction formations. But in general it is necessary to separate from each other sublimation and reaction formation as two diverse processes. Sublimation may also result through other and simpler mechanisms.

of latency and delay, we shall return to reality and state that such a utilization [54] of the infantile sexuality represents an ideal bringing up from which the development of the individual usually deviates in some measure and often very considerably. A portion of the sexual manifestation which has withdrawn from sublimation occasionally breaks through, or a sexual activity remains throughout the whole duration of the latency period until the reinforced breaking through of the sexual impulse in puberty. Insofar as they have paid any attention to infantile sexuality, the educators behave as if they shared our views concerning the formation of the moral forces of defense at the cost of sexuality and as if they knew that sexual activity makes the child uneducable; for the educators consider all sexual manifestations of the child as an "evil" in the face of which little can be accomplished. We have, however, every reason for directing our attention to those phenomena so much feared by the educators, for we expect to find in them the solution of the primitive formation of the sexual impulse.

THE MANIFESTATIONS OF INFANTILE SEXUALITY

THUMB-SUCKING. For reasons which we shall discuss later we shall take as a model of the infantile sexual manifestations thumb-sucking (pleasure-sucking), to which the Hungarian pediatrist Lindner has devoted an excellent essay.[9]

Thumb-sucking, which manifests itself in the nursing baby and which may be continued till maturity or throughout life, consists in a rhythmic repetition of sucking contact with the mouth (the lips), wherein the purpose of taking nourishment is excluded. A part of the lip itself, the tongue, which is another preferable skin region within reach, and even the big toe—may be taken as objects for sucking. Simultaneously, there is also a desire to grasp things, which manifests itself in a rhythmical pulling of the earlobe and which may cause the child to grasp a part of another person (generally the ear) for the same purpose. The pleasure-sucking is connected with an entire exhaustion of attention and leads to sleep or even to a

[9] *Jahrbuch für Kinderheilkunde,* N. F., XIV, 1879.

motor reaction [55] in the form of an orgasm.[10] Pleasure-sucking is often combined with a rubbing contact with certain sensitive parts of the body, such as the breast and external genitals. It is by this road that many children go from thumb-sucking to masturbation.

Lindner himself clearly recognized the sexual nature of this activity, and openly emphasized it. In the nursery thumb-sucking is often treated in the same way as any other sexual "naughtiness" of the child. A very strong objection was raised against this view by many pediatrists and neurologists which in part is certainly due to the confusion between the terms "sexual" and "genital." This contradiction raises the difficult question, which cannot be avoided, namely, in what general traits do we wish to recognize the sexual expression of the child. I believe that the association of the manifestations into which we have gained an insight through psychoanalytic investigation justifies us in claiming thumb-sucking as a sexual activity, and through it directly the essential features of infantile sexual activities can be studied.[11]

AUTOEROTISM. It is our duty here to arrange this state of affairs differently. Let us insist that the most striking character of this sexual activity is that the impulse is not directed against other persons but that it gratifies itself on its own body; to use [56] the happy term invented by Havelock Ellis, we shall say that it is autoerotic.[12]

[10] This already shows what holds true for the whole life, namely, that sexual gratification is the best hypnotic. Most nervous insomnias are traced to lack of sexual gratification. It is also known that unscrupulous nurses calm crying children to sleep by stroking their genitals.

[11] In 1919 a Dr. Galant in the *Neurolog. Zentralbl.*, No. 20, under the title "Das Lütscherli," published the confession of a grown-up girl who had not given up this childish sexual activity and described the pleasure of thumb-sucking as completely analogous to a sexual gratification, especially to that of a kiss from her lover. "Not all kisses equal thumb-sucking, no, no, by no means all. One cannot describe the enjoyment that goes through the entire body when one sucks one's thumb; one is far from this world; one is absolutely satisfied and supremely lucky. It is a wonderful feeling. One only wishes quiet; quiet that nothing can interrupt. It is simply indescribably wonderful; one feels no pain, no sorrow, and oh! one is transported into another world."

[12] H. Ellis has utilized the term "autoerotic" somewhat differ-

It is, moreover, clear that the action of the thumb-sucking child is determined by the fact that it seeks a pleasure which has already been experienced and is now remembered. Through the rhythmic sucking on a portion of the skin or mucous membrane it finds the gratification in the simplest way. It is also easy to conjecture on what occasions the child first experienced this pleasure which it now strives to renew. The first and most important activity in the child's life, the sucking from the mother's breast (or its substitute), must have acquainted it with this pleasure. We would say that the child's lips behaved like an *erogenous zone* and that the excitement through the warm stream of milk was really the cause of the pleasurable sensation. To be sure, the gratification of the erogenous zone was at first united with the gratification of taking nourishment. He who sees a satiated child sink back from the mother's breast, and fall asleep with reddened cheeks and blissful smile, will have to admit that this picture remains as typical of the expression of sexual gratification in later life. But the desire for repetition of the sexual gratification is separated from the desire for taking nourishment; a separation which becomes unavoidable with the appearance of the teeth when the nourishment is no longer sucked in but chewed. [57] The child does not make use of a strange object for sucking but prefers its own skin because it is more convenient, because it thus makes itself independent of the outer world which it cannot yet control, and because in this way it creates for itself, as it were, a second, even if an inferior, erogenous zone. This inferiority of this second region urges it later to seek the same parts, the lips of another person. ("It is a pity that I cannot kiss myself," might be attributed to it.)

Not all children suck their thumbs. It may be assumed that it is found only in children in whom the erogenous significance of the lip zone is constitutionally reenforced. Children in whom this is retained are habitual kissers as adults and show a tendency to perverse kissing, or as men they have a marked

---

ently. He expresses the idea of a stimulus which does not come from the outside but rather from within. For psychoanalysis it is not the genesis but the relationship to the object which is of most significance.

desire for drinking and smoking. But if repression comes into play they experience disgust for eating and evince hysterical vomiting. By virtue of the community of the lip zone the repression encroaches upon the impulse of nourishment. Many of my female patients showing disturbances in eating, such as *globus hystericus*, choking sensations, and vomiting, have been energetic thumb-suckers during infancy.

In the thumb-sucking or pleasure-sucking we have already been able to observe the three essential characters of an infantile sexual manifestation. The latter has its origin in conjunction with a bodily function which is very important for life, it does not yet know any sexual object, it is *autoerotic* and its sexual aim is under the control of an *erogenous zone*. Let us assume for the present that these characters also hold true for most of the other activities of the infantile sexual impulse.

THE SEXUAL AIM OF THE INFANTILE SEXUALITY

CHARACTER OF THE EROGENOUS ZONES. From the example of thumb-sucking we may gather a great many points useful for the distinguishing of an erogenous zone. It is a portion of skin [58] or mucous membrane in which the stimuli produce a feeling of pleasure of definite quality. There is no doubt that the pleasure-producing stimuli are governed by special determinants which we do not know. The rhythmic characters must play some part in them, and this strongly suggests an analogy to tickling. It does not, however, appear so certain whether the character of the pleasurable feeling evoked by the stimulus can be designated as "peculiar," and in what part of this peculiarity the sexual factor exists. Psychology is still groping in the dark when it concerns matters of pleasure and pain, and the most cautious assumption is therefore the most advisable. We may perhaps later come upon reasons which seem to support the peculiar quality of the sensation of pleasure.

The erogenous quality may adhere most notably to definite regions of the body. As is shown by the example of thumb-sucking, there are predestined erogenous zones. But the same example also shows that any other region of skin or mucous membrane may assume the function of an erogenous zone; it must therefore carry along a certain adaptability. The production of the sensation of pleasure therefore depends more on the quality of the stimulus than on the nature of the bodily region. The thumb-sucking child looks around on his body and selects any portion of it for pleasure-sucking, and becoming accustomed to it, he then prefers it. If he accidentally strikes upon a predestined region, such as breast, nipple, or genitals, it naturally has the preference. A quite analogous tendency to displacement is again found in the symptomatology of hysteria. In this neurosis the repression mostly concerns the genital zones proper; these in turn transmit their excitation to the other erogenous zones, usually dormant in mature life, which then behave exactly like genitals. But besides this, just as in thumb-sucking, any other region of the [59] body may become endowed with the excitation of the genitals and raised to an erogenous zone. Erogenous and hysterogenous zones show the same characters.[13]

THE INFANTILE SEXUAL AIM. The sexual aim of the infantile impulse consists in the production of gratification through the proper excitation of this or that selected erogenous zone. In order to leave a desire for its repetition this gratification must have been previously experienced, and we may be sure that nature has devised definite means so as not to leave this occurrence to mere chance.[14] The arrangement which has fulfilled this purpose for the lip zone we have already discussed; it is the simultaneous connection of this part of the body with the taking of nourishment. We shall also meet other similar mechanisms as sources of sexuality. The state of desire for repetition of gratification can be recognized through a peculiar feeling of tension which in itself is rather of a painful character, and through a centrally determined feeling of itching or sensitiveness which is projected into the

[13] Further reflection and the valuation of other observations lead me to attribute the quality of erotism to all parts of the body and inner organs. See later, on narcissism.

[14] The use of teleological forms of thought in biological explanations can hardly be avoided even though it is recognized that in individual cases one is not secure against error.

peripheral erogenous zone. The sexual aim may therefore be formulated as follows: the chief object is to substitute for the projected feeling of sensitiveness in the erogenous zone that outer stimulus which removes the feeling of sensitiveness by evoking the feeling of gratification. This external stimulus consists usually in a manipulation which is analogous to sucking.

It is in full accord with our physiological knowledge if the desire happens to be awakened also peripherally through an actual [60] change in the erogenous zone. The action is puzzling only to some extent as one stimulus for its suppression seems to want another applied to the same place.

THE MASTURBATIC SEXUAL MANIFESTATIONS [15]

It is a matter of great satisfaction to know that there is nothing further of greater importance to learn about the sexual activity of the child after the impulse of one erogenous zone has become comprehensible to us. The most pronounced differences are found in the action necessary for the gratification, which consists in sucking for the lip zone and which must be replaced by other muscular actions according to the situation and nature of the other zones.

THE ACTIVITY OF THE ANAL ZONE. Like the lip zone the anal zone is, through its position, adapted to conduct the sexuality to the other functions of the body. It should be assumed that the erogenous significance of this region of the body was originally very large. Through psychoanalysis one finds, not without surprise, the many transformations that are normally undertaken with the usual excitations emanating from here and that this zone often retains for life a considerable fragment of genital irritability.[16] The intestinal catarrhs

[15] Compare here the very comprehensive but confusing literature on onanism, e.g., Rohleder, *Die Masturbation*, 1899. Cf. also the pamphlet "Die Onanie," which contains the discussion of the Vienna Psychoanalytic Society, Wiesbaden, 1912.

[16] Compare here the essay on "Charakter und Analerotic" and "Ueber Triebumsetzungen inbesondere der Analerotik" [G. A., V]. Both are in English in *Collected Papers*, II (Hogarth Press, London). Cf. also Brill, *Psychoanalysis*, Chap. XIII, "Anal Eroticism and Character" (W. B. Saunders, Philadelphia).

so frequently during infancy produce intensive irritations in this zone, and we often hear it said that intestinal catarrh at this delicate age causes "nervousness." In later neurotic diseases they exert a definite influence on the symptomatic expression of the neurosis, placing at its disposal the whole sum of intestinal disturbances. Considering the erogenous significance of the anal zone which has been retained at least in transformation, one should not laugh at the hemorrhoidal influences to which the old medical literature attached so much weight in the explanation of neurotic states. [61]

Children utilizing the erogenous sensitiveness of the anal zone can be recognized by their holding back of fecal masses until through accumulation there result violent muscular contractions; the passage of these masses through the anus is apt to produce a marked irritation of the mucous membrane. Besides the pain this must produce also a sensation of pleasure. One of the surest premonitions of later eccentricity or nervousness is when an infant obstinately refuses to empty his bowel when placed on the chamber by the nurse and reserves this function at its own pleasure. It does not concern him that he will soil his bed; all he cares for is not to lose the subsidiary pleasure while defecating. The educators have again the right inkling when they designate children who withhold these functions as bad. The content of the bowel, which is an exciting object to the sexually sensitive surface of mucous membrane, behaves like the precursor of another organ which does not become active until after the phase of childhood. In addition it has other important meanings to the nursling. It is evidently treated as an additional part of the body; it represents the first "donation," the disposal of which expresses the pliability while the retention of it can express the spite of the little being toward its environment. From the idea of "donation" he later gains the meaning of the "babe" which according to one of the infantile sexual theories is acquired through eating and is born through the bowel.

The retention of fecal masses, which is at first intentional in order to utilize them, as it were, for masturbatic excitation of the anal zone, is at least one of the roots of constipation so frequent in neuropaths. [62] The whole significance of the anal zone is mirrored in the fact that there are but few neurotics who have not their special scatologic customs, ceremonies, and so on, which they retain with cautious secrecy.[17]

Real masturbatic irritation of the anal zone by means of the fingers, evoked through either centrally or peripherally supported itching, is not at all rare in older children.

THE ACTIVITY OF THE GENITAL ZONE. Among the erogenous zones of the child's body there is one which certainly does not play the main role and which cannot be the carrier of earliest sexual feeling—which, however, is destined for great things in later life. In both male and female it is connected with the voiding of urine (penis, clitoris), and in the former it is enclosed in a sack of mucous membrane, probably in order not to miss the irritations caused by the secretions which may arouse the sexual excitement at an early age. The sexual activities of this erogenous zone, which belongs to the real genitals, are the beginning of the later normal sexual life.

Owing to the anatomical position, the overflowing of secretions, the washing and rubbing of the body, and to certain accidental excitements (the wandering of intestinal worms in the girl), [63] it happens that the pleasurable feeling which these parts of the body are capable of producing makes itself noticeable to the child even during the sucking age, and thus awakens desire for its repetition. When we review all the actual arrangements, and bear in mind that the measures for cleanliness have the same effect as the uncleanliness itself,

[17] In a contribution ("'Anal' und 'Sexual'" *Imago,* IV, 1916, abstract in *Psychoanalytic Review,* 9, 255, 1916) which has deepened extraordinarily our understanding of the significance of anal erotism, Lou Andreas-Salomé has pointed out that the history of the first forbidding which comes to the child, i.e., the forbidding of obtaining pleasure from anal activities and its products, is of immeasurable significance for its entire development. The little child through such an occasion must get an inkling of an environment antagonistic to his instinct stirrings, must learn from these strangers his own nature, and then accomplish the first repression of his pleaure possibilities. That which is "anal" from then on remains as a symbol for everything that must be pushed aside, to be cut out of life. The later demands of a pure separation of the anal and genital processes are opposed to the close anatomical and functional analogies and relations between both. The genital apparatus remains a neighbor to the cloaca "ist ihr beim Weibe sogar nur abgemietet" (in the woman it is merely sublet to it).

we can then scarcely mistake nature's intention, which is to establish the future primacy of these erogenous zones for the sexual activity through the infantile onanism from which hardly an individual escapes. The action of removing the stimulus and setting free the gratification consists in a rubbing contiguity with the hand or in a certain previously formed pressure reflex effected by the closure of the thighs. The latter procedure seems to be the more primitive and is by far the more common in girls. The preference for the hand in boys already indicates what an important part of the male sexual activity will be accomplished in the future by the impulse to mastery (Bemächtigungstrieb).[18]

It can only help toward clearness if I state that the infantile masturbation should be divided into three phases. The first phase belongs to the nursing period, the second to the short flourishing period of sexual activity at about the fourth year; only the third corresponds to the one which is often considered exclusively as onanism of puberty.

SECOND PHASE OF CHILDHOOD MASTURBATION. Infantile onanism seems to disappear after a brief time, but it may continue uninterruptedly till puberty, and this represents the first marked deviation from the development desirable for civilized man. At some time during childhood after the nursing period, the sexual impulse of the genitals rewakens and continues active for some time until it is again suppressed, or it may continue without interruption. The possible relations [64] are very diverse and can be elucidated only through a more precise analysis of individual cases. The details, however, of this *second* infantile sexual activity leave behind the profoundest (unconscious) impressions in the person's memory; if the individual remains healthy they determine his character and if he becomes sick after puberty they determine the symptomatology of his neurosis.[19] In the latter case it is found that this

[18] Unusual techniques in the performance of onanism seem to point to the influence of a prohibition against onanism which has been overcome.

[19] Why neurotics, when conscience stricken, regularly connect it with their onanistic activity, as was only recently recognized by Bleuler, is a problem which still awaits an exhaustive analysis. The greatest and most important factor of this determination may well be the fact that masturbation truly represents the execution of the

sexual period is forgotten and the conscious reminiscences pointing to them are displaced; I have already mentioned that I should like to connect the normal infantile amnesia with this infantile sexual activity. By psychoanalytic investigation it is possible to bring to consciousness the forgotten material, and thereby to remove a compulsion which emanates from the unconscious psychic material.

THE RETURN OF INFANTILE MASTURBATION. The sexual excitation of the nursing period returns during the designated years of childhood as a centrally determined tickling sensation demanding onanistic gratification, or as a pollution-like process which, analogous to the pollution of maturity, may attain gratification without the aid of any action. The latter case is more frequent in girls and in the second half of childhood; its determinants are not well understood, but it often, though not regularly, seems to have as a basis a period of early active onanism. The symptomatology of this sexual manifestation is poor; the genital apparatus is still undeveloped and all signs are therefore displayed by the urinary apparatus which is, so to say, the guardian of the genital apparatus. Most of the so-called bladder disturbances of this period are of a sexual nature; whenever the enuresis nocturnal does not represent an epileptic attack it corresponds to a pollution. [65]

The return of the sexual activity is determined by inner and outer causes which can be conjectured from the formation of the symptoms of neurotic diseases and definitely revealed by psychoanalytic investigations. The internal causes will be discussed later; the accidental outer causes attain at this time a great and permanent significance. As the first outer cause there is the influence of seduction which prematurely treats the child as a sexual object; under conditions favoring impressions this teaches the child the gratification of the genital zones, and thus usually forces it to repeat this gratification in onanism. Such influences can come from adults or other children. I cannot admit that I overestimated its frequency or its significance in my contributions to the etiology of hysteria,[20]

---

entire infantile sexuality and is therefore enabled to take over this fixated sense of guilt.

[20] Freud, *Selected Papers on Hysteria and Other Psychoneuroses,*

though I did not know then that normal individuals may have the same experiences in their childhood, and hence placed a higher value on seductions than on the factors found in the sexual constitution and development.[21] It is quite obvious that no seduction is necessary to awaken the sexual life of the child, that such an awakening may come on spontaneously from inner sources.

POLYMORPHOUS-PERVERSE DISPOSITION. It is instructive to know that under the influence of seduction the child may become polymorphous-perverse and may be misled into all sorts of transgressions. This shows that it carries along the adaptation for them in its disposition. The formation of such perversions [66] meets but slight resistance because the psychic dams against sexual transgressions, such as shame, loathing and morality—which depend on the age of the child—are not yet erected or are only in the process of formation. In this respect the child perhaps does not behave differently from the average uncultured woman in whom the same polymorphous-perverse disposition exists. Such a woman may remain sexually normal under usual conditions, but under the guidance of a clever seducer she will find pleasure in every perversion and will retain the same as her sexual activity. The same polymorphous or infantile disposition fits the prostitute for her professional activity, and in an enormous number of prostitutes and of women to whom we must attribute an adaptation for prostitution, even if they do not follow this calling, it is absolutely impossible not to recognize in their uniform disposition for all perversions the universal and primitive human.

3d edition, translated by A. A. Brill, Nervous and Mental Disease Monograph Series, No. 4.

[21] Havelock Ellis, in an appendix to his study, *The Sexual Impulse*, 1903, gives a number of autobiographic reports of normal persons dealing with their first sexual feelings in childhood and the causes of the same. These reports naturally show the deficiencies due to infantile amnesia; they do not cover the prehistoric time in the sexual life and therefore must be supplemented by psychoanalysis of individuals who became neurotic. Notwithstanding this, these reports are valuable in more than one respect, and information of a similar nature has urged me to modify my etiological assumption as mentioned in the text.

PARTIAL IMPULSES. For the rest, the influence of seduction does not aid us in unraveling the original relations of the sexual impulse, but rather confuses our understanding of the same, inasmuch as it prematurely supplies the child with the sexual object at a time when the infantile sexual impulse does not yet evince any desire for it. We must admit, however, that the infantile sexual life, though mainly under the control of erogenous zones, also shows components in which from the very beginning other persons are regarded as sexual objects. Among these we have the impulses for looking and showing off, and for cruelty, which manifest themselves somewhat independently of the erogenous zones and which only later enter into intimate relationship with the sexual life; but along with the erogenous sexual activity they are noticeable even in the infantile years as separate and independent strivings. The little child is, above all, shameless, and during its early years it evinces definite pleasure in displaying its body and especially its sexual organs. A counterpart to this [67] desire, which is to be considered as perverse, the curiosity to see other person's genitals, probably appears first in the later years of childhood when the hindrance of the feeling of shame has already reached a certain development. Under the influence of seduction the looking perversion may attain great importance for the sexual life of the child. Still, from my investigations of the childhood years of normal and neurotic patients, I must conclude that the impulse for looking can appear in the child as a spontaneous sexual manifestation. Small children, whose attention has once been directed to their own genitals—usually by masturbation—are wont to progress in this direction without outside interference and to develop a vivid interest in the genitals of their playmates. As the occasion for the gratification of such curiosity is generally afforded during the gratification of both excrementitious needs, such children become voyeurs and are zealous spectators at the voiding of urine and feces of others. After this tendency has been repressed, the curiosity to see the genitals of others (one's own or those of the other sex) remains as a tormenting desire which in some neurotic cases furnishes the strongest motive power for the formation of symptoms.

The cruelty component of the sexual impulse develops in the child with still greater independence of those sexual activities which are connected with erogenous zones. Cruelty is especially near the childish character, since the inhibition which restrains the impulse to mastery before it causes pain to others—that is, the capacity for sympathy—develops comparatively late. As we know, a thorough psychological analysis of the impulse has not as yet been successfully accomplished; we may assume that the cruel feelings emanate from the impulse to mastery and appear at a period in the sexual life before the genitals have taken on their later role. [68] It then dominates a phase of the sexual life, which we shall later describe as the pregenital organization. Children who are distinguished for evincing especial cruelty to animals and playmates may be justly suspected of intensive and premature sexual activity in the erogenous zones; and in a simultaneous prematurity of all sexual impulses the erogenous sexual activity surely seems to be primary. The absence of the barrier of sympathy carries with it the danger that the connections between cruelty and the erogenous impulses formed in childhood cannot be broken in later life.

An erogenous source of the passive impulse for cruelty (masochism) is found in the painful irritation of the gluteal region which is familiar to all educators since the confessions of J. J. Rousseau. This has justly caused them to demand that physical punishment, which usually concerns this part of the body, should be withheld from all children in whom the libido might be forced into collateral roads by the later demands of cultural education.[22] [69]

[22] The assertions here mentioned concerning infantile sexuality were justified in 1905, in the main through the results of psychoanalytic investigations in adults. Direct observation of the child could not at the time be utilized to its full extent and resulted only in individual indications and valuable confirmations. Since then it has become possible through the analysis of some cases of nervous disease in the delicate age of childhood to gain a direct understanding of the infantile psychosexuality. I can point with satisfaction to the fact that direct observation has fully confirmed the conclusion drawn from psychoanalysis, and thus furnishes good evidence for the reliability of the latter method of investigation. Moreover, the "Analysis of a Phobia in a Five-Year-Old Boy" (*Jahrbuch*, Bd. I [G. S., VIII], in English in *Collected Papers*,

STUDY OF INFANTILE SEXUALITY

INQUISITIVENESS. About the same time when the sexual life of the child reaches its first rich development, from the age of three to the age of five, the beginnings of that activity ascribed to the impulse for knowledge and investigation set in. The desire for knowledge can neither be reckoned among the elementary instinctive components nor can it be altogether subsumed under sexuality. Its activity corresponds on the one hand to a sublimated form of acquisition; on the other hand the energy with which it works comes from the looking impulse. Its relations to the sexual life, however, are of particular importance, for we have learned from psychoanalysis that the inquisitiveness of children is attracted to sexual problems unusually early and in unexpectedly intensive manner; indeed, it perhaps may first be awakened by the sexual problems.

THE RIDDLE OF THE SPHINX. They are not theoretical but practical interests which start the work of the child's investigation activity. The menace to the conditions of his existence through the actual or expected arrival of a new child, the fear of losing care and love which is connected with this event, cause the child to become thoughtful and sagacious. Corresponding with the history of this awakening, the first problem with which it occupies itself is not the question as to the difference between the sexes, but the riddle: Where do children come from? In a distorted form, which can easily be unraveled, this is the same riddle which was proposed by the Theban Sphinx. The fact of the two sexes is usually first accepted by the child without struggle and hesitation. It is quite

---

Vol. III [Hogarth Press, London]) has taught us something new for which psychoanalysis had not prepared us, to wit, that sexual symbolism, the representation of the sexual by nonsexual objects and relations—reaches back into the years when the child is first learning to master the language. My attention has also been directed to a deficiency in the above-cited statement which for the sake of clearness described any conceivable separation between the two phases of autoerotism and object love as a temporal separation. From the cited analysis (as well as from the work of Bell noted, see p. 35, note 2,) we learn that children from three to five are capable of evincing a very strong object-selection which is accompanied by strong affects.

natural for the male child to presuppose in all persons it knows a genital like his own, and to find it impossible to harmonize the lack of it with his conception of others. [70]

THE CASTRATION COMPLEX AND PENIS ENVY. This conviction is energetically adhered to by the boy and stubbornly defended against the contradictions which soon result, and are only given up after severe internal struggles (castration complex). The substitute formations of this lost penis on the part of the woman play a great role in the formation of many perversions.[23]

The assumption of the same (male) genital in all persons is the first of the remarkable and consequential infantile sexual theories. It is of little help to the child when biological science agrees with his preconceptions and recognizes the feminine clitoris as the real substitute for the penis. The little girl does not react with similar refusals when she sees the differently formed genital of the boy. She is immediately prepared to recognize it, and soon becomes envious of the penis; this envy reaches its highest point in the consequentially important wish that she were a boy.

BIRTH THEORIES. Many people can remember distinctly how intensely they interested themselves, in the prepubescent period, in the question where children came from. The anatomical solutions at that time read very differently; the children come out of the breast or are cut out of the body, or the navel opens itself to let them out.[24] Outside of analysis one only seldom remembers the investigation corresponding to the early childhood years; it had long merged into repression but its results were thoroughly uniform. One gets children by eating something special (as in the fairy tale), and they are born through the bowel like a passage. These infantile theories

[23] One has the right to speak also of a castration complex with women. Male and female children form the theory that originally the woman, too, had a penis, which has been lost through castration. The conviction finally won that the woman has no penis often leaves behind it in the male a lasting depreciation of the other sex.

[24] The wealth of sexual theories in these later years of childhood is very great. Only a few examples are given in the text.

recall the structures in the animal kingdom, especially do they recall the cloaca of the types which stand lower than the mammals. [71]

SADISTIC CONCEPTION OF THE SEXUAL ACT. If children at so tender an age become witnesses of the sexual act between adults, for which an occasion is furnished by the conviction of the people that little children cannot understand anything sexual, they cannot help conceiving the sexual act as a kind of maltreating or overpowering, that is, it impresses them in a sadistic sense. Psychoanalysis teaches us also that such an early childhood impression contributes much to the disposition for a later sadistic displacement of the sexual aim. Besides this, children also occupy themselves with the problem of what the sexual act consists in or, as they grasp it, of what marriage consists, and seek the solution of the mystery usually in an intimacy carried on through the functions of urination and defecation.

THE TYPICAL FAILURE OF THE INFANTILE SEXUAL INVESTIGATION. It can be stated in general about infantile sexual theories that they are reproductions of the child's own sexual constitution and that despite their grotesque mistakes they evince more understanding of the sexual processes than is credited to their creators. Children also perceive the pregnancy of the mother and know how to interpret it correctly; the stork fable is very often related before auditors who confront it with a deep but mostly mute suspicion. Inasmuch as two elements remain unknown to infantile sexual investigation, namely, the role of the fructifying semen and the existence of the female genital opening—precisely the same points in which the infantile organization is still backward—the effort of the infantile mind regularly remains fruitless, and ends in a renunciation which not infrequently leaves a lasting injury to the desire for knowledge. The sexual investigation of these early childhood years is always conducted alone; it signifies the first step toward independent orientation in the world, and causes a marked estrangement between the child and the persons of his environment who formerly enjoyed its full confidence. [72]

DEVELOPMENTAL PHASES OF THE SEXUAL ORGANIZATION

As characteristic of the infantile sexuality we have hitherto emphasized the fact that it is essentially autoerotic (it finds its object in its own body) and that its individual partial impulses, which on the whole are unconnected and independent of one another, are striving for the acquisition of pleasure. The goal of this development forms the so-called normal sexual life of the adult in whom the acquisition of pleasure has been put into the service of the function of propagation, and the partial impulses, under the primacy of one single erogenous zone, have formed a firm organization for the attainment of the sexual aim in a strange sexual object.

PREGENITAL ORGANIZATIONS. The study, with the help of psychoanalysis, of the inhibitions and disturbances in this course of development now permits us to recognize additions and primary stages of such organizations of the partial impulses which likewise furnish a sort of sexual regime. These phases of the sexual organization are normally smoothly passed through and will be recognizable only by mere indications. Only in pathological cases do they become active and discernible to gross observation.

We shall call the organizations of the sexual life in which the genital zones have not yet assumed the dominating role the *pregenital phase.* So far we have become acquainted with two of them which recall reversions to early animal states.

One of the first of such pregenital sexual organizations is the *oral*, or, if one will, the cannibalistic. Here the sexual activity is not yet separated from the taking of nourishment, and the contrasts within it are not yet differentiated. The object of the one activity is also that of the other; the sexual aim consists in the *incorporation* of the object into one's own body, the prototype of that which later as *identification* plays such an important psychic role. As a remnant of this fictitious phase of organization forced on us by pathology we can consider thumb-sucking. [73] Here the sexual activity became separated from the nourishment activity, and the strange object was given up in favor of one from his own body.[25]

A second pregenital phase is the sadistic-anal organization. Here the contrasts which run through the whole sexual life are already developed, but cannot yet be designated as *masculine* and *feminine*, but must be called *active* and *passive*. The activity is supplied by the musculature of the body through the mastery impulse; the erogenous mucous membrane of the bowel manifests itself above all as an organ with a passive sexual aim; for both strivings there are objects present, which however do not merge together. Besides them there are other partial impulses which are active in an autoerotic manner. The sexual polarity and the strange object can thus already be demonstrated in this phase. The organization and subordination under the function of propagation are still lacking.[26]

AMBIVALENCE. This form of the sexual organization could be retained throughout life and continue to draw to itself a large part of the sexual activity. The prevalence of sadism and the role of the cloaca of the anal zone stamps it with an exquisitely archaic impression. As another characteristic belonging to it we can mention the fact that the contrasting pair of impulses are developed in almost the same manner, a situation which was happily designated by Bleuler by the term *ambivalence*.

The assumption of the pregenital organization of the sexual life rests on the analysis of the neuroses and can scarcely be appreciated without a knowledge of these. [74] We have a right to expect that continual analytic efforts will furnish us

[25] Cf. concerning remnants of this phase in adult neurotics the work of Abraham, "Investigations Regarding the Earliest Pregenital Stage of Development of the Libido" (*Int. Zeit. f. Psa.*, IV, 1916). In a later work (*Versuch einer Entwicklungsgeschichte der Libido*, 1924) Abraham subdivided both this oral phase and the later sadistic-anal one into two parts, for which the different behavior toward the object is characteristic. In English in *Selected Papers*, Int. Psa. Library 13 (Hogarth Press, 1927).

[26] In the second of the two studies, Abraham calls attention to the fact that the anus arises from the primitive mouth of the embryonic form which appears as a biological prototype of the psychosexual development.

with still more disclosures concerning the structure and development of the normal sexual function.

To complete the picture of the infantile sexual life one must add further that frequently or regularly an object selection takes place even in a childhood which is as characteristic as the one we have represented for the phase of development of puberty. This object selection proceeds in such a manner that all the sexual strivings proceed in the direction of one person in whom they wish to attain their aim. This is then the nearest approach to the definitive formation of the sexual life after puberty that is possible in childhood. It differs from the latter only in the fact that the collection of the partial impulses and their subordination to the primacy of the genitals is very imperfectly or not at all accomplished in childhood. The establishment of this primacy in the service of reproduction is therefore the last phase through which sexual development passes.[27]

THE TWO PERIODS OF OBJECT SELECTION. That the object selection takes place in two periods, or in two shifts, can be spoken of as a typical occurrence. The first shift has its origin between the age of three and five years, and is brought to a stop or to retrogression by the latency period; it is characterized by the infantile nature of its sexual aims. The second shift starts with puberty and determines the definitive formation of the sexual life.

The fact of the double object selection which is essentially due [75] to the effect of the latency period, becomes most significant for the disturbance of this terminal state. The results of the infantile object selection reach into the later period; they are either preserved as such or are even refreshed

[27] I have later (1925) altered this in that I have interpolated a third phase into the development of the child after the two pregenital organizations, one that indeed deserves the name of a genital one, which reveals a sexual object and a measure of convergence of the sexual strivings upon this object, but differs in one essential point from the definitive organization of sexual maturity. That is, it knows only one sort of genital, the male. I have therefore called it the *phallic* stage of organization ("Die infantile Genitalorganisation," *Int. Zeit f. Psa.*, IX, 1925; G. S., V). Its biological prototype, according to Abraham, is the homogeneous genital anlage of the embryo undifferentiated for either sex.

at the time of puberty. But due to the development of the repression which takes place between the two phases they turn out as unutilizable. The sexual aims have become softened and now represent what we can designate as the *tender* streams of the sexual life. Only psychoanalytic investigation can demonstrate that behind this tenderness, such as honoring and esteeming, there is concealed the old sexual strivings of the infantile partial impulses which have now become useless. The object selection of the pubescent period must renounce the infantile objects and begin anew as a sensuous stream. The fact that the two streams do not meet often enough has as a result that one of the ideals of the sexual life, namely, the union of all desires in one object, cannot be attained.

THE SOURCES OF INFANTILE SEXUALITY

In our effort to follow up the origins of the sexual impulse, we have thus far found that the sexual excitement originates (*a*) as an imitation of a gratification which has been experienced in conjunction with other organic processes; (*b*) through the appropriate peripheral stimulation of erogenous zones; (*c*) and as an expression of some "impulse," like the looking and cruelty impulses, the origin of which we do not yet fully understand. The psychoanalytic investigation of later life which leads back to childhood and the contemporary observation of the child itself cooperate to reveal to us still other regularly flowing sources of the sexual excitement. The observation of childhood has the disadvantage of treating easily misunderstood material, while psychoanalysis is made difficult by the fact that it can [76] reach its objects and conclusions only by great detours; still, the united efforts of both methods achieve a sufficient degree of positive understanding.

In investigating the erogenous zones we have already found that these skin regions show merely the special exaggeration of a form of sensitiveness which is to a certain degree found over the whole surface of the skin. It will therefore not surprise us to learn that certain forms of general sensitiveness in the skin can be ascribed to very distinct erogenous action. Among these we shall above all mention the temperature sensitiveness; this will perhaps prepare us for the understanding of the therapeutic effects of warm baths.

MECHANICAL EXCITATION. We must, moreover, describe here the production of sexual excitation by means of rhythmic mechanical shaking of the body. There are three kinds of exciting influences: those acting on the sensory apparatus of the vestibular nerves, those acting on the skin, and those acting on the deep parts, such as the muscles and joints. The sexual excitation produced by these influences seems to be of a pleasurable nature—it is worth emphasizing that for some time we shall continue to use indiscriminately the terms "sexual excitement" and "gratification" leaving the search for an explanation of the terms to a later time—and that the pleasure is produced by mechanical stimulation is proved by the fact that children are so fond of play involving passive motion, like swinging or flying in the air, and repeatedly demand its repetition.[28] As we know, rocking is regularly used in putting restless children to sleep. The shaking sensation experienced in wagons and railroad trains exerts such a fascinating influence on older children that all boys, at least at [77] one time in their lives, want to become conductors and drivers. They are wont to ascribe to railroad activities an extraordinary and mysterious interest, and during the age of fantastic activity (shortly before puberty) they utilize these as a nucleus for exquisite sexual symbolisms. The desire to connect railroad traveling with sexuality apparently originates from the pleasurable character of the sensation of motion. When the repression later sets in and changes so many of the childish likes into their opposites, these same persons as adolescents and adults then react to the rocking and rolling with nausea and become terribly exhausted by a railroad journey, or they show a tendency to attacks of anxiety during the journey, and by becoming obsessed with railroad phobia they protect themselves against a repetition of the painful experiences.

This also fits in with the not as yet understood fact that the concurrence of fear with mechanical shaking produces the severest hysterical forms of traumatic neurosis. It may at least

[28] Some persons can recall that the contact of the moving air in swinging caused them direct sexual pleasure in the genitals.

be assumed that inasmuch as even a slight intensity of these influences becomes a source of sexual excitement, the action of an excessive amount of the same will produce a profound disorder in the sexual mechanism.

MUSCULAR ACTIVITY. It is well known that the child has need for strong muscular activity, from the gratification of which it draws extraordinary pleasure. Whether this pleasure has anything to do with sexuality, whether it includes in itself sexual satisfaction, or can be the occasion of sexual excitement, all this may be refuted by critical consideration, which will probably be directed also to the position just taken that the pleasure in the sensations of passive movement are of sexual character or that they are sexually exciting. The fact remains, however, that a number of persons report that they experienced the first signs of excitement in their genitals during fighting or wrestling with playmates, in which situation, besides the general muscular exertion, [78] there is an intensive contact with the opponent's skin, which also becomes effective. The desire for muscular contest with a definite person, like the desire for word contest in later years, is a good sign that the object selection has been directed toward this person. "Was sich liebt, das neckt sich."[29] In the promotion of sexual excitement through muscular activity, we might recognize one of the sources of the sadistic impulse. The infantile connection between fighting and sexual excitement acts in many persons as a determinant for the future preferred course of their sexual impulse.[30]

AFFECTIVE PROCESSES. The other sources of sexual excitement in the child are open to less doubt. Through contemporary observations, as well as through later investigations, it is easy to ascertain that all more intensive affective processes, even excitements of a terrifying nature, encroach upon sex-

[29] "Those who love each other tease each other."

[30] The analyses of neurotic disturbances of walking and of agoraphobia remove all doubt as to the sexual nature of the pleasure of motion. As everybody knows, modern cultural education utilizes sports to a great extent in order to turn youth away from sexual activity; it would be more proper to say that it replaces the sexual pleasure by motion pleasure, and forces the sexual activity back upon one of its autoerotic components.

uality; this can at all events furnish us with a contribution to the understanding of the pathogenic action of such emotions. In the schoolchild, fear of a coming examination or exertion expended in the solution of a difficult task can become significant for the breaking through of sexual manifestations as well as for his relations to the school, inasmuch as under such excitements a sensation often occurs urging him to touch the genitals, or leading to a pollution-like process with all its disagreeable consequences. The behavior of children at school, which is so often mysterious to the teacher, ought surely to be considered in relation with their germinating sexuality. The sexually exciting influence of some painful affects, such as fear, shuddering, and horror, is felt by a great many people throughout life and readily explains why so many [79] seek opportunities to experience such sensations, provided that certain accessory circumstances (as under imaginary circumstances in reading, or in the theater) suppress the earnestness of the painful feeling.

If we might assume that the same erogenous action also reaches the intensive painful feelings, especially if the pain be toned down or held at a distance by a subsidiary determination, this relation would then contain the main roots of the masochistic-sadistic impulse, into the manifold composition of which we are gaining a gradual insight.[31]

INTELLECTUAL WORK. Finally, it is evident that mental application or the concentration of attention on an intellectual accomplishment will result, especially often in youthful persons, but in older persons as well, in a simultaneous sexual excitement, which may be looked upon as the only justified basis for the otherwise so doubtful etiology of nervous disturbances from mental "overwork."

If we now, in conclusion, review the evidences and indications of the sources of the infantile sexual excitement, which have been reported neither completely nor exhaustively, we may lay down the following general laws as suggested or established. It seems to be provided in the most generous manner that the process of sexual excitement—the nature of which certainly remains quite mysterious to us—should be set

[31] The so-called "erogenic" masochism.

in motion. The factor making this provision in a more or less direct way is the excitation of the sensible surfaces of the skin and sensory organs, while the most immediate exciting influences are exerted on certain parts which are designated as erogenous zones. The criterion in all these sources of sexual excitement is really the quality of the stimuli, though the factor of intensity (in pain) is not entirely unimportant. But in addition to this there are arrangements in the organism which induce sexual excitement as a subsidiary action [80] in a large number of inner processes as soon as the intensity of these processes has arisen above certain quantitative limits. What we have designated as the partial impulses of sexuality are either directly derived from these inner sources of sexual excitation or composed of contributions from such sources and from erogenous zones. It is possible that nothing of any considerable significance occurs in the organism that does not contribute its components to the excitement of the sexual impulse.

It seems to me at present impossible to shed more light and certainty on these general propositions, and for this I hold two factors responsible; first, the novelty of this manner of investigation, and second, the fact that the nature of the sexual excitement is entirely unfamiliar to us. Nevertheless, I shall not forbear speaking about two points which promise to open wide prospects in the future.

DIVERSE SEXUAL CONSTITUTIONS. (*a*) We have considered above the possibility of establishing the manifold character of congenital sexual constitutions through the diverse formation of the erogenous zones; we may now attempt to do the same in dealing with the indirect sources of sexual excitement. We may assume that, although these different sources furnish contributions in all individuals, they are not all equally strong in all persons and that a further contribution to the differentiation of the diverse sexual constitution will be found in the preferred development of the individual sources of sexual excitement.[32]

[32] An undeniable result of these outlines is that every individual may be spoken of as oral-, anal-, urethral-erotic, etc., and that the finding of these psychical complexes entails no judgment as to ab-

THE PATHS OF OPPOSITE INFLUENCES. (*b*) Since we are now dropping the figurative manner of expression hitherto employed, [81] by which we spoke of *sources* of sexual excitement, we may now assume that all the connecting ways leading from other functions to sexuality must also be passable in the reverse direction. For example, if the lip zone, the common possession of both functions, is responsible for the fact that sexual gratification originates during the taking of nourishment, the same factor offers also an explanation for the disturbances in the taking of nourishment if the erogenous functions of the common zone are disturbed. As soon as we know that concentration of attention may produce sexual excitement, it is quite natural to assume that acting on the same path, but in a contrary direction, the state of sexual excitement will be able to influence the availability of the voluntary attention. A good part of the symptomatology of the neuroses which I trace of disturbance of sexual processes manifests itself in disturbances of the other nonsexual bodily functions, and this hitherto incomprehensible action becomes less mysterious if it represents only the counterpart of the influences controlling the production of the sexual excitement.

However, the same paths through which sexual disturbances encroach upon the other functions of the body must in health be supposed to serve another important function. It must be through these paths that the attraction of the sexual motive powers to other than sexual aims, the sublimation of sexuality, is accomplished. We must conclude with the admission that very little is definitely known concerning the paths beyond the fact that they exist and that they are probably passable in both directions.

---

normality or a neurosis. That which separates the normal from the abnormal is but a relative increase in the single components of the sexual impulses and what course they may take during development.

Contribution III

THE TRANSFORMATIONS OF PUBERTY

With the beginning of puberty changes set in which transform the infantile sexual life into its definite normal form. [82] Hitherto the sexual impulse has been preponderantly autoerotic; it now finds the sexual object. Thus far it has manifested itself in single impulses and in erogenous zones seeking a certain pleasure as a single sexual aim. A new sexual aim now appears for the production of which all partial impulses cooperate, while the erogenous zones subordinate themselves to the primacy of the genital zone.[1] As the new sexual aim assigns very different functions to the two sexes their sexual developments now part company. The sexual development of the man is more consistent and easier to understand, while in the woman there even appears a form of regression. The normality of the sexual life is guaranteed only by the exact concurrence of the two streams directed to the sexual object and sexual aim. It is like the piercing of a tunnel from opposite sides.

The new sexual aim in the man consists in the discharging of [83] the sexual products; it is not contradictory to the former sexual aim, that of obtaining pleasure; on the contrary, the highest amount of pleasure is connected with this final act in the sexual process. The sexual impulse now enters into the service of the function of propagation; it becomes, so to say, altruistic. If this transformation is to succeed its process must be adjusted to the original dispositions and all the peculiarities of the impulses.

Just as on every other occasion where new connections and

[1] The differences will be emphasized in the schematic representation given in the text. To what extent the infantile sexuality approaches the definitive sexual organization through its object selection has been discussed previously.

compositions are to be formed in complicated mechanisms, here, too, there is a possibility for morbid disturbances if the new order of things does not get itself established. All morbid disturbances of the sexual life may justly be considered as inhibitions of development.

THE PRIMACY OF THE GENITAL ZONES AND THE FOREPLEASURE

From the course of development as described we can clearly see the issue and the end aim. The intermediary transitions are still quite obscure, and many a riddle will have to be solved in them.

The most striking process of puberty has been selected as its most characteristic; it is the manifest growth of the external genitals, which have shown a relative inhibition of growth during the latency period of childhood. Simultaneously the inner genitals develop to such an extent as to be able to furnish sexual products or to receive them for the purpose of forming a new living being. A most complicated apparatus is thus utilized which waits to be claimed.

This apparatus can be set in motion by stimuli, and observation teaches that the stimuli can effect it in three ways: from the outer world through the familiar erogenous zones; from the inner [84] organic world by ways still to be investigated; and from the psychic life, which merely represents a depository of external impressions and a receptacle of inner excitations. The same result follows in all three cases, namely, a state which can be designated as "sexual excitation" and which manifests itself in psychic and somatic signs. The psychic sign consists in a peculiar feeling of tension of a most urgent character, and among the manifold somatic signs the many changes in the genitals stand first. They have a definite meaning, that of readiness; they constitute a preparation for the sexual act (the erection of the penis and the glandular activity of the vagina).

SEXUAL TENSION. The character of the tension of sexual excitation is connected with a problem the solution of which is as difficult as it would be important for the conception of the sexual process. Despite all divergence of opinion regarding it in psychology, I must firmly maintain that a feeling of tension must carry with it the character of displeasure. For me it is conclusive that such a feeling carries with it the impulse to alter the psychic situation, and acts incitingly, which is quite contrary to the nature of perceived pleasure. But if we ascribe the tension of the sexual excitation to the feelings of displeasure, we encounter the fact that it is undoubtedly pleasurably perceived. The tension produced by sexual excitation is everywhere accompanied by pleasure; even in the preparatory changes of the genitals there is a distinct feeling of satisfaction. What relation is there between this unpleasant tension and this feeling of pleasure?

Everything relating to the problem of pleasure and pain touches one of the weakest spots of present-day psychology. We shall try if possible to learn something from the determination of the case in question and to avoid encroaching on the problem as a whole. [85] Let us first glance at the manner in which the erogenous zones adjust themselves to the new order of things.[2] An important role devolves upon them in the preparation of the sexual excitation. The eye, which is very remote from the sexual object, is most often in position, during the relations of object wooing, to become attracted by that particular quality of excitation, the motive of which we designate as beauty in the sexual object. The excellencies of the sexual object are therefore also called "attractions." This attraction is on the one hand already connected with pleasure, and on the other hand it either results in an increase of the sexual excitation or in an evocation of the same where it is still wanting. The effect is the same if the excitation of another erogenous zone, for example, the touch of the hand, is added to it. There is on the one hand the feeling of pleasure which soon becomes enhanced by the pleasure from the preparatory changes, and on the other hand there is a further increase of

[2] See an effort toward the solution of this question in the introductory discussion of my paper "Das ökonomische Problem der Masochismus," (*Int. Zeit. f. Psa.*, 1924, G. S., V). In English in Vol. II, *Collected Papers* (Hogarth Press, London).

the sexual tension which soon changes into a most distinct feeling of displeasure if it cannot proceed to more pleasure.

Another case will perhaps be clearer; let us, for example, take the case where an erogenous zone, like a woman's breast, is excited by touching in a person who is not sexually excited at the time. This touching in itself evokes a feeling of pleasure, but it is also best adapted to awaken sexual excitement which demands still more pleasure. How it happens that the perceived pleasure evokes the desire for greater pleasure is the real problem.

FOREPLEASURE MECHANISM. But the role which devolves upon the erogenous zones is clear. What applies to one applies to all. They are all utilized to furnish a certain amount of pleasure through their own proper excitation, which increases the tension [86] and which is in turn destined to produce the necessary motor energy in order to bring the sexual act to a conclusion. The last part but one of this act is again a suitable excitation of an erogenous zone; that is, the genital zone proper of the glans penis is excited by the object most fit for it, the mucous membrane of the vagina, and through the pleasure furnished by this excitation it now produces reflexly the motor energy which conveys to the surface the sexual substance. This last pleasure is highest in its intensity, and differs from the earliest ones in its mechanism. It is altogether produced through discharge; it is altogether gratification pleasure, and the tension of the libido temporarily dies away with it.

It does not seem to me unjustified to fix by name the distinction in the nature of these pleasures, the one through the excitation of the erogenous zones, and the other through the discharge of the sexual substance. In contradistinction to the endpleasure, or pleasure of gratification of sexual activity, we can properly designate the first as *forepleasure*. The forepleasure is then the same as that furnished by the infantile sexual impulse, though on a reduced scale; while the *endpleasure* is new and is probably connected with determinations which first appear at puberty. The formula for the new function of the erogenous zones reads as follows: they are utilized for the purpose of making possible the production of the greater pleasure of gratification by means of the forepleasure which is gained from them as in infantile life.

I have recently been able to elucidate another example from a quite different realm of the psychic life, in which likewise a greater feeling of pleasure is achieved by means of a lesser feeling of pleasure which thereby acts as an alluring premium. We had there also the opportunity of entering more deeply into the nature of pleasure.[3] [87]

DANGERS OF THE FOREPLEASURE. However, the connection of forepleasure with the infantile life is strengthened by the pathogenic role which may devolve upon it. In the mechanism through which the forepleasure is expressed there exists an obvious danger to the attainment of the normal sexual aim. This occurs if it happens that there is too much forepleasure and too little tension in any part of the preparatory sexual process. The motive power for the furthr continuation of the sexual process then escapes, the whole road becomes shortened, and the preparatory action in question takes the place of the normal sexual aim. Experience shows that such a hurtful condition is determined by the fact that the erogenous zone concerned or the corresponding partial impulse has already contributed an unusual amount of pleasure in infantile life. If other factors favoring fixation are added, a compulsion readily results for the later life which prevents the forepleasure from arranging itself into a new combination. Indeed, the mechanism of many perversions is of such nature; they merely represent a lingering at a preparatory act of the sexual process.

The failure of the function of the sexual mechanism through the fault of the forepleasure is generally avoided if the primacy of the genital zones has also already been sketched out in infantile life. The preparations of the second half of childhood (from the eighth year to puberty) really seem to favor this. During these years the genital zones behave almost as

[3] See my work *Wit and Its Relation to the Unconscious*, translated by A. A. Brill (Dodd, Mead & Co., New York): "The forepleasure gained by the technique of wit is utilized for the purpose of setting free a greater pleasure by the removal of inner inhibitions."

at the age of maturity; they are the seat of exciting sensations and of preparatory changes if any kind of pleasure is experienced through the gratification of other erogenous zones; although this effect remains aimless, that is, it contributes nothing toward the continuation of the sexual process. Besides the pleasure of gratification a certain amount of sexual tension appears even in infancy, though it is less constant and less abundant. We can now understand also why we had a perfectly good reason for saying, [88] in the discussion of the sources of sexuality, that the process in question acts as sexual gratification as well as sexual excitement. We note that on our way toward the truth we have at first enormously exaggerated the distinction between the infantile and the mature sexual life, and we therefore supplement what has been said with a correction. The infantile manifestations of sexuality determine not only the deviations from the normal sexual life but also the normal formations of the same.

THE PROBLEM OF SEXUAL EXCITEMENT

It remains entirely unexplained whence the sexual tension comes which originates simultaneously with the gratification of erogenous zones and what is its nature.[4] The obvious supposition that this tension originates in some way from the pleasure itself is not only improbable in itself but untenable, inasmuch as during the greatest pleasure which is connected with the voiding of sexual substance there is no production of tension but rather a removal of all tension. Hence, pleasure and sexual tension can be only indirectly connected.

THE ROLE OF SEXUAL SUBSTANCES. Aside from the fact that only the discharge of the sexual substance can normally put an end to the sexual excitement, there are other essential facts which bring the sexual tension into relation with the sex-

[4] It is extremely informing that the German language in the use of the word *Lust* takes cognizance of the role of preparatory sexual excitement, here mentioned, which at the same time delivers a part of satisfaction and a share of the sexual tension. *Lust* has a double meaning, and signifies not only the sensation of sexual tension (*Ich habe Lust* (=I have the desire)=*ich möchte; ich verspüre den Drang* (I would like to, I am aware of the tension), but also that of its gratification.

ual products. In a life of continence the sexual activity is wont to discharge the sexual substance at night during pleasurable dream hallucinations of a sexual act, this discharge coming at changing but not at entirely capricious intervals; and the following interpretation of this process—the nocturnal pollution—can hardly [89] be rejected, namely, that the sexual tension which brings about a substitute for the sexual act by the short hallucinatory road is a function of the accumulated semen in the reservoirs for the sexual products. Experiences with the exhaustibility of the sexual mechanism speak for the same thing. Where there is no stock of semen it is not only impossible to accomplish the sexual act, but there is also a lack of excitability in the erogenous zones, the suitable excitation of which can evoke no pleasure. We thus discover incidentally that a certain amount of sexual tension is itself necessary for the excitability of the erogenous zones.

One would thus be forced to the assumption, which if I am not mistaken is quite generally adopted, that the accumulation of sexual substance produces and maintains the sexual tension. The pressure of these products on the walls of their receptacles acts as an excitant on the spinal center, the state of which is then perceived by the higher centers which then produce in consciousness the familiar feeling of tension. If the excitation of erogenous zones increases the sexual tension, it can only be due to the fact that the erogenous zones are connected with these centers by previously formed anatomical connections. They increase there the tone of the excitation, and with sufficient sexual tension they set in motion the sexual act, and with insufficient tension they merely stimulate a production of the sexual substance.

The weakness of the theory which one finds adopted, for example, in v. Krafft-Ebing's description of the sexual process, lies in the fact that it has been formed for the sexual activity of the mature man and pays too little heed to three kinds of relations which should also have been elucidated. We refer to the relations as found in the child, in the woman, and in the castrated male. In none of the three cases can we speak of an accumulation of sexual products in the same sense as in the man, which naturally renders difficult the general application of this scheme; still it may be [90] admitted without any further ado that ways can be found to justify the subordination of even these cases. Nevertheless one should be cautious about burdening the factor of accumulation of sexual products with actions which it seems incapable of supporting.

OVERESTIMATION OF THE INTERNAL GENITALS. That sexual excitement can be independent to a considerable extent of the production of sexual substance seems to be shown by observations on castrated males, in whom the libido sometimes escapes the injury caused by the operation, although the opposite behavior, which is really the motive for the operation, is usually the rule. It is therefore not at all surprising, as C. Rieger puts it, that the loss of the male germ glands in maturer age should exert no new influence of the psychic life of the individual. The germ glands are really not the sexuality, and the experience with castrated males only verifies what we had long before learned from the removal of the ovaries, namely, that it is impossible to do away with the sexual character by removing the germ glands. To be sure, castration performed at a tender age, before puberty, comes nearer to this aim, but it would seem in this case that besides the loss of the sexual glands we must also consider the inhibition of development and other factors which are connected with that loss.

CHEMICAL THEORIES. Animal experimentation by the removal of the gonads (testicles and ovaries) and the corresponding varying transplantations of such organs in vertebrates (see Lipschütz's work *(Die Pubersätsdürse und ihre Wirkungen)* have finally thrown a partial light upon the origins of sexual excitement and thereby gone still further back into the significance of an eventual heaping up of cellular sexual products. Experimentally it has been possible (E. Steinach) to change a male into a female, and vice versa, in that the psychosexual behavior of the animal corresponds to the somatic sexual characters and changes with them at the same time. [91] This sex-determining influence does not, however, proceed from those portions of the gonads concerned with the production of spermatozoa or ovules but rather from the interstitial cells which are therefore designated (by Lipschütz) as "puberty glands." It is quite possible that further research will show that the puberty glands are hermaphroditic whereby the doctrine concerning the bisexuality of higher animals may be anatomically grounded, and furthermore it is still possible that they are not the only organs which have to do with the production of sexual excitement and with the sexual characters. At all events these newer findings relate themselves to what we alrealy know of the role played by the thyroid in sexuality. We may now believe that in the interstitial tissues of the gonads special chemical substances are produced which, taken up in the bloodstream, permit the charge of definite parts of the central nervous system with sexual tension. Such a transformation of a toxic stimulus into a particular organic stimulus we are already familiar with from other toxic products introduced into the body from without. To treat, if only hypothetically, the complexities of the pure toxic and the physiologic stimulations which result in the sexual processes is not now our appropriate task. To be sure, I attach no value to this special assumption and I shall be quite ready to give it up in favor of anothr, provided its original character, the emphasis on the sexual chemism, were preserved. For this apparently arbitrary statement is supported by a fact which, though little heeded, is most noteworthy. The neuroses which can be traced only to disturbances of the sexual life show the greatest clinical resemblance to the phenomena of intoxication and abstinence which result from the habitual introduction of pleasure-producing poisonous substances (alkaloids). [92]

THE LIBIDO THEORY

These assumptions concerning the chemical basis of the sexual excitement are in full accord with the auxiliary conception which we formed for the purpose of mastering the psychic manifestations of the sexual life. We have laid down the concept of *libido* as that of a force of variable quantity which has the capacity of measuring processes and transformations in the spheres of sexual excitement. This libido we distinguished from the energy which is to be generally adjudged to the psychic processes with reference to its special origin, and thus we attribute to it also a qualitative character. In separating libidinous from other psychic energy we give expression to the assumption that the sexual processes of the organism are differentiated from the nutritional processes through a special chemism. The analyses of perversions and psychoneuroses have taught us that this sexual excitement is furnished not only from the so-called sexual parts alone but from all organs of the body. We thus formulate for ourselves the concept of a libido quantum whose psychic representative we designate as the *ego-libido;* the production, increase, distribution, and displacement of this ego-libido will offer the possible explanation for the observed psychosexual phenomena.

But this ego-libido becomes conveniently accessible to psychoanalytic study only when the psychic energy is employed in the charging [cathexis] of sexual objects, that is, when it becomes *object-libido.* Then we see it as it concentrates and fixes itself on objects, or as it leaves those objects and passes over to others, from which position it directs the individual's sexual activity; that is, it leads to partial and temporary extinction of the libido. Psychoanalysis of the so-called transference neuroses (hysteria and compulsion neurosis) offers us here a reliable insight. [93]

Concerning the fates of the object-libido, we also state that it is withdrawn from the object, that it is preserved floating in special states of tension, and is finally taken back into the ego, so that it again becomes ego-libido. In contradistinction to the object-libido we also call the ego-libido *narcissistic libido.* From psychoanalysis we look over the boundary, which we are not permitted to pass, into the activity of the narcissistic libido and thus form an idea of the relations between the two.[5] The narcissistic or ego-libido appears to us as the great reservoir from which the energy for the investment (cathexis) of the object is sent out and into which it is drawn back again, while the narcissistic libido investment of the ego appears to us as the realized primitive state in the first child-

[5] This limitation is not as valid as it once was inasmuch as other neuroses besides the "transference neuroses" have become to a greater degree accessible to psychoanalysis.

hood, which becomes hidden only by the later emissions of the libido, and is retained at the bottom behind them.

The task of a libido theory of neurotic and psychotic disturbances would have for its object to express in terms of the libido-economics all observed phenomena and disclosed processes. It is easy to divine that the greater significance would attach thereby to the destinies of the ego-libido, especially where it would be the question of explaining the deeper psychotic disturbances. The difficulty then lies in the fact that the means of our investigation, psychoanalysis, at present gives us definite information[6] only concerning the transformation of the object-[95] libido, but cannot distinguish without further study the ego-libido from the other effective energies in the ego.[7] The libido theory may therefore for the present be pursued only by the path of speculation. All that has been gained from psychoanalytic observation thus far is relinquished if one follows the procedure of C. G. Jung in subtilizing the concept of the libido, permitting it to coincide with psychic instinctive energy in its totality.

The separation of the sexual instinctive excitements from the others and thus the restriction of the concept libido to the former find strong support in the previously discussed assumption of a particular chemistry of the sexual function.

DIFFERENTIATION BETWEEN MAN AND WOMAN

It is known that the sharp differentiation of the male and female character originates at puberty, and it is the resulting difference which, more than any other factor, decisively influences the later development of personality. To be sure, the male and female dispositions are easily recognizable even in infantile life; thus the development of sexual inhibitions (shame, loathing, sympathy, and so on,) ensues earlier and with less resistance in the little girl than in the little boy. The tendency to sexual repression certainly seems much greater, and where partial impulses of sexuality are noticed they show a prefer-

[6] See previous citations.

[7] Cf. "Zur Einführung des Narzismus," *Jahrbuch der Psychoanalyse,* VI, 1913. The term "narcissism" was not devised, as there incorrectly stated, by Naecke, but by H. Ellis.

ence for the passive form. But the autoerotic activity of the erogenous zones is the same in both sexes, and it is this agreement that removes the possibility of a sex differentiation in childhood as it appears after puberty. In respect to the autoerotic and masturbatic sexual manifestations, it may be asserted that the sexuality of the little girl has entirely a male character. Indeed, if one could give a more definite content to the terms "masculine" and "feminine," one might advance the opinion that the libido is regularly and lawfully of a masculine nature, whether in the man or in the woman; [95] and if we consider its object, this may be either the man or the woman.[8]

Since becoming acquainted with the aspect of bisexuality I hold this factor as here decisive, and I believe that without taking into account the factor of bisexuality it will hardly be possible to understand the actually observed sexual manifestations in man and woman.

THE LEADING ZONES IN MAN AND WOMAN. Further than this I can add only the following. The chief erogenous zone in

[8] It is necessary to make clear that the conceptions "masculine" and "feminine," whose content seems so unequivocal to the ordinary meaning, belong to the most confused terms in science and can be cut up into at least three paths. One uses masculine and feminine at times in the sense of activity and passivity, again, in the biological sense, and then also in the sociological sense. The first of these three meanings is the essential one and the only one utilizable in psychoanalysis. It agrees with the masculine designation of the libido in the text above, for the libido is always active even when it is directed to a passive aim. The second, the biological significance of masculine and feminine, is the one which permits the clearest determination. Masculine and feminine are here characterized by the presence of semen or ovum and through the functions emanating from them. The activity and its secondary manifestations, like stronger-developed muscles, aggression, a greater intensity of libido, are as a rule soldered to the biological masculinity but not necessarily connected with it, for there are species of animals in which these qualities are attributed to the female. The third, the sociological meaning, receives its content through the observation of the actual existing male and female individuals. The result of this in man is that there is no pure masculinity or femininity either in the biological or psychological sense. On the contrary every individual person shows a mixture of his own biological sex characteristics with the biological traits of the other sex and a union of activity and passivity; this is the case whether these psychological characteristic features depend on the biological or whether they are independent of it.

the female child is the clitoris, which is homologous to the male penis. All I have been able to discover concerning masturbation in little girls concerned the clitoris and not those other external genitals which are so important for the later sexual functions. With few exceptions I myself doubt whether the female child can be seduced to anything but clitoris masturbation. The frequent spontaneous discharges of sexual excitement in little girls manifest themselves in a twitching of the clitoris, and its frequent erections enable the [96] girl to understand correctly even without any instruction the sexual manifestations of the other sex; they simply transfer to the boys the sensations of their own sexual processes.

If one wishes to understand how the little girl becomes a woman, he must follow up the further destinies of this clitoris excitation. Puberty, which brings to the boy a great advance of libido, distinguishes itself in the girl by a new wave of repression which especially concerns the clitoris sexuality. It is a part of the male sexual life that sinks into repression. The reenforcement of the sexual inhibitions produced in the woman by the repression of puberty causes a stimulus in the libido of the man and forces it to increase its capacity; with the height of the libido there is a rise in the overestimation of the sexual, which can be present in its full force only when the woman refuses and denies her sexuality. If the sexual act is finally submitted to and the clitoris becomes excited, its role is then to conduct the excitement to the adjacent female parts, and in this it acts like a chip of pinewood which is utilized to set fire to the harder wood. It often takes some time for this transference to be accomplished, during which the young wife remains anesthetic. This anesthesia may become permanent if the clitoris zone refuses to give up its excitability, a condition brought on by abundant activities in infantile life. It is known that anesthesia in women is often only apparent and local. They are anesthetic at the vaginal entrance but not at all unexcitable through the clitoris or even through other zones. Besides these erogenous causes of anesthesia there are also psychic causes likewise determined by the repression. [97]

If the transference of the erogenous excitability from the

clitoris to the vagina has succeeded, the woman has thus changed her leading zone for the future sexual activity; the man on the other hand retains his from childhood. The main determinants for the woman's preference for the neuroses, especially for hysteria, lie in this change of the leading zone as well as in the repression of puberty. These determinants are therefore most intimately connected with the nature of femininity.

OBJECT-FINDING

While the primacy of the genital zones is being established through the processes of puberty, and the erected penis in the man imperiously points toward the new sexual aim, that is, toward the penetration of a cavity which excites the genital zone, the object-finding, for which also preparations have been made since early childhood, becomes consummated on the psychic side. While the very incipient sexual gratifications are still connected with the taking of nourishment, the sexual impulse has a sexual object outside its own body in the mother's breast. This object it loses later, perhaps at the very time when it becomes possible for the child to form a general picture of the person to whom the organ granting him the gratification belongs. The sexual impulse later regularly becomes autoerotic, and only after overcoming the latency period is there a resumption of the original relation. It is not without good reason that the suckling of the child at its mother's breast has become a model for every amour. The object-finding is really a refinding.[9] [98]

THE SEXUAL OBJECT OF THE NURSING PERIOD. However, even after the separation of the sexual activity from the taking of nourishment, there still remains from this first and most important of all sexual relations an important share, which prepares the object selection and assists in reestablishing the

[9] Psychoanalysis teaches that there are two paths of object-finding; the first is the one discussed in the text which is guided by the early infantile prototypes. The second is the narcissistic which seeks its own body and finds it in someone else. The latter is of particularly great significance for the pathological outcomes, but does not fit into the connection treated here.

lost happiness. Throughout the latency period the child learns to love other persons who assist it in its helplessness and gratify its wants; all this follows the model and is a continuation of the child's infantile relations to his wet nurse. One may perhaps hesitate to identify the tender feelings and esteem of the child for his foster-parents with sexual love; I believe, however, that a more thorough psychological investigation will establish this identity beyond any doubt. The intercourse between the child and its foster-parents is for the former an inexhaustible source of sexual excitation and gratification of erogenous zones, especially since the parents—or as a rule the mother—supplies the child with feelings which originate from her own sexual life; she pats it, kisses it, and rocks it, plainly taking it as a substitute for a full-valued sexual object.[10] The mother would probably be terrified if it were explained to her that all her tenderness awakens the sexual impulse of her child and prepares its future intensity. She considers her actions as asexually "pure" love, for she carefully avoids causing more irritation to the genitals of the child than is indispensable in caring for the body. [99] But as we know, the sexual impulse is not awakened by the excitation of genital zones alone. What we call tenderness will someday surely manifest its influence on the genital zones also. If the mother better understood the high significance of the sexual impulse for the whole psychic life and for all ethical and psychic activities, the enlightenment would spare her all reproaches. By teaching the child to love she only fulfills her function; for the child should become a fit man with energetic sexual needs, and accomplish in life all that the impulse urges the man to do. Of course, too much parental tenderness becomes harmful because it accelerates the sexual maturity, and also because it "spoils" the child and makes it unfit temporarily to renounce love or be satisfied with a smaller amount of love in later life. One of the surest premonitions of later nervousness is the fact that the child shows itself insatiable in its demands for parental tenderness; on the other hand, neuropathic parents, who

[10] Those to whom this conception appears "wicked" may read Havelock Ellis's treatise on the relations between mother and child which expresses almost the same ideas (*The Sexual Impulse*, p. 16).

usually display a boundless tenderness, often with their caressing awaken in the child a disposition for neurotic diseases. This example at least shows that neuropathic parents have nearer ways than inheritance by which they can transfer their disturbances to their children.

INFANTILE ANXIETY. The children themselves behave from their early childhood as if their attachment to their foster-parents were of the nature of sexual love. The fear of children is originally nothing but an expression for the fact that they miss the beloved person. They therefore meet every stranger with fear; they are afraid of the dark because they cannot see the beloved person, and are calmed if they can grasp that person's hand. The effect of childish fears and of the terrifying stories told by nurses is overestimated if one blames the latter for producing the fear in children. Children who are predisposed to fear absorb these stories, which make no impression whatever upon others; and only such children are predisposed to fear whose sexual impulse [100] is excessive or prematurely developed, or has become exigent through pampering. The child behaves here like the adult, that is, it changes its libido into fear when it cannot bring it to gratification, and the grown-up who becomes neurotic on account of ungratified libido behaves in his anxiety like a child; he fears when he is alone, that is, without a person of whose love he believes himself sure and who can calm his fears by means of the most childish measures.[11]

If the tenderness of the parents for the child has luckily

[11] For the explanation of the origin of the infantile fear I am indebted to a three-year-old boy whom I once heard calling from a dark room: "Auntie, talk to me; I am afraid because it is dark." "How will that help you?" answered the aunt. "You cannot see anyhow." "That's nothing," answered the child, "if someone talks, then it becomes light." He was, as we see, not afraid of the darkness; he was afraid because he missed the person he loved, and he could promise to calm down as soon as he was assured of her presence. That neurotic anxiety originates from the libido, representing a transformation product of the same, also being related to it, as vinegar is to wine, is one of the most significant results of psychoanalytic research. For further discussion of these problems see my *Introductory Lectures to Psychoanalysis* (1917, trustworthy translation by Joan Rivière, London, 1922), where even a final explanation has not been achieved.

failed to awaken the sexual impulse of the child prematurely, that is, before the physical determinations for puberty appear, and if that awakening has not gone so far as to cause an unmistakable breaking through of the psychic excitement into the genital system, it can then fulfill its task and direct the child at the age of maturity in the selection of the sexual object. It would, of course, be most natural for the child to select as the sexual object that person whom it has loved since childhood with, so to speak, a suppressed libido.[12] But owing to the delay of sexual maturity, time has been gained for the erection beside the sexual inhibitions of the incest barrier, that moral prescription which explicitly excludes from the object selection the beloved person of infancy or blood relation. The observance of this [101] barrier is above all a demand of cultural society which must guard against the absorption by the family of those interests which it needs for the production of higher social units. Society, therefore, uses every means to loosen those family ties in every individual, especially in the boy, which are authoritative in childhood only.[13]

The object selection, however, is first accomplished in the imagination, and the sexual life of the maturing youth has hardly any escape except indulgence in fantasies or ideas which are not destined to be brought to execution.[14] In the

[12] Cf. here what is said on page 60 concerning the object selection of the child, the "tender stream."

[13] The incest barrier probably belongs to the historical acquisitions of humanity, and like other moral taboos it must be fixed in many individuals through organic heredity. (Cf. my work *Totem and Taboo*, 1913, G. S. X. [English translation by A. A. Brill.]) Psychoanalytic studies show, however, how intensively the individual struggles with the incest temptations during his development and how frequently he puts them into fantasies and even into reality.

[14] The fantasies of puberty join themselves to the infantile sexual investigation abandoned in childhood, perhaps also reach back a little into the latency period. They may be retained wholly or in great part unconsciously, and therefore frequently do not permit of exact location in time. They are of great significance in the origin of many symptoms inasmuch as they furnish precisely the prestages of these; that is, they determine the forms in which the repressed libido components find their satisfaction. In the same way they are the patterns for the fantasies of the night, which come into consciousness as dreams. Dreams are often nothing else than

fantasies of all [102] persons the infantile inclinations, now reenforced by somatic emphasis, reappear, and among them one finds in regular frequency and in the first place the sexual feeling of the child for the parents. This has usually already been differentiated by the sexual attraction, the attraction of the son for the mother and of the daughter for the father.[15] Simultaneously with the overcoming and rejection of these distinctly incestuous fantasies there occurs one of the most important as well as one of the most painful psychic accomplishments of puberty; it is the breaking away from the parental authority, through which alone is formed that opposition between the new and old generations which is so important for cultural progress. Many persons are detained at each of the stations in the course of development through which the indi-

---

revivals of such fantasies under the influence of, and leaning upon, a day stimulus left over from the waking life ("day remnants").

Certain of the sexual fantasies of puberty stand out distinguished as quite universal in occurrence and to a very great degree independent of the experience of the individual. Thus the fantasies of spying upon parental coitus; of early seduction through beloved persons; of the threat of castration; fantasies of the mother's womb, whose content is the being within the womb and the things experienced there; and the so-called "family romance," in which the growing child reacts to the difference in his attitude toward the parents now and in childhood. O. Rank has shown in his book *The Myth of the Birth of the Hero* (1909), as regards the latter example, the close relations of these fantasies to the myth (English translation by Jelliffe, in Monograph Series, No. 18).

One says rightly that the Œdipus complex is the nuclear complex of the neuroses, that it represents the essential part in the content of the neuroses. It is the culminating point of infantile sexuality, which through its aftereffects decisively influences the sexuality of the adult. The task before each new human being is to master the Œdipus complex; one who cannot do this falls into a neurosis. Progress in psychoanalytic work has resulted in an ever clearer picture of the significance of the Œdipus complex; its recognition has become the shibboleth which distinguishes the followers of psychoanalysis from its opponents.

In another work (*Das Trauma der Geburt,* 1924) Rank has carried the fixation to the mother back to the embryonic past and so pointed out the biological foundation of the Œdipus complex. He derives the incest barrier, differing from what has just been said, from the traumatic effect of the birth anxiety.

[15] Compare the description concerning the inevitable relation in the Œdipus legend in *The Interpretation of Dreams,* p. 222, translated by A. A. Brill (The Macmillan Co., New York, and Allen & Unwin, London) (G. S. III, IV).

vidual must pass; and accordingly there are persons who never overcome the parental authority and never, or very imperfectly, withdraw their affection from their parents. They are mostly girls, who, to the delight of their parents, retain their full infantile love far beyond puberty, and it is instructive to find that in their married life these girls are incapable of fulfilling their duties to their husbands. They make cold wives and remain sexually anesthetic. This shows that the apparently nonsexual love for the parents and the sexual love are nourished from the same source, that is, that the first merely corresponds to an infantile fixation of the libido.

The nearer we come to the deeper disturbances of the psychosexual development, the more easily we can recognize the [103] evident significance of the incestuous object-selection. As a result of sexual rejection there remains in the unconscious of the psychoneurotic a great part of the whole of the psychosexual activity for object finding. Girls with an excessive need for affection and an equal horror for the real demands of the sexual life experience an uncontrollable temptation on the one hand to realize in life the ideal of the asexual love and on the other hand to conceal their libido under an affection which they may manifest without self-reproach; this they do by clinging for life to the infantile attraction for their parents or brothers or sisters which has been repressed in puberty. With the help of the symptoms and other morbid manifestations, psychoanalysis can trace their unconscious thoughts and translate them into the conscious, and thus easily show to such persons that they are in love with their consanguinous relations in the popular meaning of the term. Likewise when a once healthy person falls sick after an unhappy love affair, the mechanism of the disease can distinctly be explained as a return of his libido to the persons preferred in his infancy.

THE AFTEREFFECTS OF THE INFANTILE OBJECT SELECTION. Even those who have happily eluded the incestuous fixation of their libido have not completely escaped its influence. It is a distinct echo of this phase of development that the first serious love of the young man is often for a mature woman and that of the girl for an older man equipped with authority—

that is, for persons who can revive in them the picture of the mother and father.[16] Generally speaking, object selection unquestionably takes place by following more freely these prototypes. The man seeks above all the memory picture of his mother as it has dominated him since the beginning of childhood; this is quite consistent with the fact that the mother, if still living, strives against this, her renewal, and meets it with hostility. In view of this significance of the [104] infantile relation to the parents for the later selection of the sexual object, it is easy to understand that every disturbance of this infantile relation brings to a head the most serious results for the sexual life after puberty. Jealousy of the lover, too, never lacks the infantile sources or at least the infantile reinforcement. Quarrels between parents and unhappy marital relations between the same determine the severest predispositions for disturbed sexual development or neurotic diseases in the children.

The infantile desire for the parents is, to be sure, the most important, but not the only trace revived in puberty which points the way to the object selection. Other dispositions of the same origin permit the man, still supported by his infancy, to develop more than one single sexual series and to form different determinations for the object selection.[17]

PREVENTION OF INVERSION. One of the tasks imposed in the object selection consists in not missing the opposite sex. This, as we know, is not solved without some difficulty. The first feelings after puberty often enough go astray, though not with any permanent injury. Dessoir has correctly called attention to the normality of the enthusiastic friendships formed by boys and girls with their own sex. The greatest force which guards against a permanent inversion of the sexual object is surely the attraction exerted by the opposite sex characters on each other. For this we can give no explanation in connec-

[16] See my study, "Ueber einen besondern Tyus der Objectwahl beim Manne," 1910 [G. S., V], English translation by Joan Rivière, *Collected Papers*, IV (Hogarth Press, London).

[17] Innumerable peculiarities of the human love-life as well as the compulsiveness of being in love itself can surely be understood only through a reference to childhood or as an effective remnant of the same.

tion with this discussion.[18] This factor, however, does not in itself suffice to exclude the inversion; [105] besides this there are surely many other supporting factors. Above all, there is the authoritative inhibition of society; experience shows that where the inversion is not considered a crime it fully corresponds to the sexual inclinations of many persons. Moreover, it may be assumed that in the man the infantile memories of the mother's tenderness, as well as that of other females who cared for him as a child, energetically assist in directing his selection to the woman, while the early sexual intimidation experienced through the father and the attitude of rivalry existing between them deflects the boy from the same sex. Both factors also hold true in the case of the girl whose sexual activity is under the special care of the mother. This results in a hostile relation to the same sex which decisively influences the object selection in the normal sense. The bringing up of boys by male persons (slaves in the ancient times) seems to favor homosexuality; the frequency of inversion in the present-day nobility is probably explained by their employment of male servants and by the scant care that mothers of that class give to their children. It happens in some hysterics that one of the parents has disappeared (through death, divorce, or estrangement), thus permitting the remaining parent to absorb all the love of the child, and in this way establishing the determinations for the sex of the person to be selected later as the sexual object; thus a permanent inversion is made possible.

[18] Here is the place to call attention to a certain fantastic but at the same time very penetrating study by Ferenczi (*Versuch einer Genitaltheorie*, 1924), in which the sexual life of higher animals is traced back to their biological evolutionary stages.

Summary

It is now time to attempt a summing up. We have started [106] from the aberrations of the sexual impulse in reference to its object and aim and have encountered the question whether these originate from a congenital predisposition, or whether they are acquired in consequence of influences from life. The answer to this question was reached through an examination of the relations of the sexual life of psychoneurotics, a numerous group not very remote from the healthy. This examination has been made through psychoanalytic investigations. We have thus found that a tendency to all perversions might be demonstrated in these persons in the form of unconscious forces revealing themselves as symptom creators, and we could say that the neurosis is, as it were, the negative of the perversion. In view of the now recognized great diffusion of tendencies to perversion, the idea forced itself upon us that the disposition to perversions is the primitive and universal disposition of the human sexual impulse, from which the normal sexual behavior develops in consequence of organic changes and psychic inhibitions in the course of maturity. We hoped to be able to demonstrate the original disposition in the infantile life; among the forces restraining the direction of the sexual impulse we have mentioned shame, loathing, and sympathy, and the social constructions of morality and authority. We have thus been forced to perceive in every fixed aberration from the normal sexual life a fragment of inhibited development and infantilism. The significance of the variations of [107] the original dispositions had to be put into the foreground, but between them and the influences of life we had to assume a relation of cooperation and not of opposition. On the other hand, as the original disposition must have been a complex one, the sexual impulse itself appeared to us as something composed of many factors, which in the perversions becomes separated, as it were, into its components. The perversions thus prove themselves to be on the one hand inhibitions, and on the other dissociations from the normal development. Both conceptions became united in the assumption that the sexual impulse of the adult, owing to the composition of the diverse feelings of the infantile life, became formed into one unit, one striving, with a single aim.

We also added an explanation for the preponderance of perversive tendencies in the psychoneurotics by recognizing in these tendencies collateral fillings of side branches caused by the shifting of the main riverbed through repression, and we then turned our examination to the sexual life of the infantile period.[19] We found it regrettable that the existence of a sexual life in infancy has been disputed and that the sexual manifestations which have been often observed in children have been described as abnormal occurrences. It rather seemed to us that the child brings along into the world germs of sexual activity and that even while taking nourishment it at the same time also enjoys a sexual gratification which it then seeks again to procure for itself through the familiar activity of "thumb-sucking.' The sexual activity of the child, however, does not develop in the same measure as its other functions, but merges first into the so-called latency period from the age of three to the age of five years. [108] The production of sexual excitation by no means ceases at this period, but continues and furnishes a stock of energy, the greater part of which is utilized for aims other than sexual; namely, on the one hand for the delivery of sexual components for social feelings, and on the other hand (by means of repression and reaction formation) for the erection of the future sexual barriers. Accordingly, the forces which are destined to hold the sexual impulse in certain tracks are built up in infancy at the expense of the greater part of the perverse sexual feelings and with the assistance of education. Another part of the infantile sexual manifestations escapes this utilization and may manifest itself

[19] This was true not only of the "negative" tendencies to perversion appearing in the neurosis, but also of the so-called positive perversions. The latter are not only to be attributed to the fixation of the infantile tendencies but also to regression to these tendencies owing to the misplacement of other paths of the sexual stream. Hence the positive perversions are also accessible to psychoanalytic therapy. (Cf. the works of Sadger, Ferenczi, and Brill.)

as sexual activity. It can then be discovered that the sexual excitation of the child flows from diverse sources. Above all gratifications originate through the adapted sensible excitation of so-called erogenous zones. For these, probably any skin region or sensory organ may serve; but there are certain distinguished erogenous zones the excitation of which by certain organic mechanisms is assured from the beginning. Moreover, sexual excitation originates in the organism, as it were, as a by-product in a great number of processes, as soon as they attain a certain intensity; this especially takes place in all strong emotional excitements even if they be of a painful nature. The excitations from all these sources do not yet unite, but they pursue their aim individually—this aim consisting merely in the gaining of a certain pleasure. The sexual impulse of childhood is therefore objectless or *autoerotic*.

Still, during infancy the erogenous zone of the genitals begins to make itself noticeable, either by the fact that like any other erogenous zone it furnishes gratification through a suitable sensible stimulus, or because in some incomprehensible way the gratification from other sources causes at the same time the sexual excitement which has a special connection with the genital zone. [109] We found cause to regret that a sufficient explanation of the relations between sexual gratification and sexual excitement, as well as between the activity of the genital zone and the remaining sources of sexuality, was not to be attained.

We have noticed through the study of neurotic disturbances that from the very beginning tendencies toward an organization of the sexual instinctive components may be recognized in infantile sexual life. The *oral erotism* stands in the foreground in a first, very early phase; a second of these "pregenital" organizations is characterized by the predominance of *sadism* and *anal erotism*, and only in a third phase (which in the child develops merely as far as the primacy of the phallus) is the sexual life determined, also through the participation of the true genital zones.

We have then been compelled to assert as one of the most striking discoveries that this early flowering of infantile sexual life (second to fifth year) also brings to maturity an object choice with all the rich psychic functioning so that the phase joined to this and corresponding to it, despite the imperfect amalgamation of the individual instinctive components and the lack of certainty in the sexual aim, must be valued as the important precursor of the later final sexual organization.

The fact that sexual development in man shows *two different periods,* namely, the interruption of this development by the latency period, has seemed to us to deserve special consideration. It appears to contain one of the conditions for fitting man to develop to a higher culture, but also for his tendency to neurosis. So far as we know, nothing analogous is demonstrable in man's animal kin. The origin of this human peculiarity would have to be sought in the primal history of the human species. [110]

We were unable to state what amount of sexual activity in childhood might be designated as normal to the extent of being incapable of further development. The character of the sexual manifestation showed itself to be preponderantly masturbatic. We, moreover, verified from experience the belief that the external influences of seduction might produce premature breaches in the latency period leading as far as the suppression of the same and that the sexual impulse of the child really shows itself to be polymorphous-perverse; furthermore, that every such premature sexual activity impairs the educability of the child.

Despite the incompleteness of our examinations of the infantile sexual life, we were subsequently forced to attempt to study the serious changes produced by the appearance of puberty. We selected two of the same as criteria, namely, the subordination of all other sources of the sexual feeling to the primacy of the genital zones, and the process of object finding. Both of them are already developed in childhood. The first is accomplished through the mechanism of utilizing the forepleasure, whereby all other independent sexual acts which are connected with pleasure and excitement become preparatory acts for the new sexual aim, the voiding of the sexual products, the attainment of which under enormous pleasure puts an end to the sexual feeling. At the same time we had to consider the differentiation of the sexual nature of man and woman, and we found that in order to become a woman a new repression is required which abolishes a piece of infantile masculinity, and prepares the woman for the change of the leading genital zones. Lastly, we found the object selection, tracing it through infancy to its revival in puberty; we also found indications of sexual inclinations on the part of the child for the parents and foster-parents, which, however, were turned away from these persons to others resembling them by the incest barriers which had been erected in the meantime. Let us finally add that during the transition period [111] of puberty the somatic and psychic processes of development proceed side by side, but separately, until with the breaking through of an intense psychic love-stimulus for the innervation of the genitals, the normally demanded unification of the erotic function is established.

FACTORS DISTURBING THE DEVELOPMENT. As we have already shown by different examples, every step on this long road of development may become a point of fixation, and every joint in this complicated structure may afford opportunity for a dissociation of the sexual impulse. It still remains for us to review the various inner and outer factors which disturb the development, and to mention the part of the mechanism affected by the disturbance emanating from them. The factors which we mention here in a series, of course, cannot all be in themselves of equal validity, and we must expect to meet with difficulties in the assigning to the individual factors their due importance.

CONSTITUTION AND HEREDITY. In the first place, we must mention here the congenital *variation of the sexual constitution,* upon which the greatest weight probably falls, but the existence of which, as may be easily understood, can be established only through its later manifestations and even then not always with great certainty. We understand by it a preponderance of one or another of the manifold sources of the sexual excitement, and we believe that such a difference of disposition must always come to expression in the final result, even if it should remain within normal limits. Of course, we can also imagine certain variations of the original disposition that even without further aid must necessarily lead to the formation of an abnormal sexual life. One can call these "degenerative" and consider them as an expression of hereditary deterioration. In this connection I have to report a remarkable fact. In more than half of the severe cases of hysteria, compulsion neuroses, and so on, which I have treated [112] by psychotherapy, I have succeeded in positively demonstrating that their fathers have gone through an attack of syphilis before marriage; they have either suffered from tabes or general paresis, or there was a definite history of lues. I expressly add that the children who were later neurotic showed absolutely no signs of hereditary lues, so that the abnormal sexual constitution was to be considered as the last offshoot of the luetic heredity. As far as it is now from my thoughts to put down a descent from syphilitic parents as a regular and indispensable etiological determination of the neuropathic constitution, I nevertheless maintain that the coincidence observed by me is not accidental and not without significance.

The hereditary relations of the positive perverts are not so well known because they know how to avoid inquiry. Still, there is reason to believe that the same holds true in the perversions as in the neuroses. We often find perversions and psychoneuroses in the different sexes of the same family, so distributed that the male members, or one of them, is a positive pervert, while the females, following the repressive tendencies of their sex, are negative perverts or hysterics. This is a good example of the substantial relations between the two disturbances which I have discovered.

FURTHER ELABORATIONS. It cannot, however, be maintained that the structure of the sexual life is rendered finally complete by the addition of the diverse components of the sexual constitution. On the contrary, qualifications continue to appear and new possibilities result, depending upon the fate experienced by the sexual streams originating from the individual sources. This *further elaboration* is evidently the final and decisive one, while the constitution described as uniform may lead to three [113] final issues. If all the dispositions assumed to be abnormal retain their relative proportion, and are strengthened with maturity, the ultimate result can only be a perverse sexual life. The analysis of such abnormally constituted dispositions has not yet been thoroughly undertaken, but we already know cases that can be readily explained in the light of these theories. Authors believe, for example, that a whole series of fixation perversions must necessarily have had as their basis a congenital weakness of the sexual impulse. The statement seems to me untenable in this form, but it becomes ingenious if it refers to a constitutional weakness of one factor in the sexual impulse, namely, the genital zone, which later in the interests of propagation accepts as a function the sum of the individual sexual activities. In this case the summation which is demanded in puberty must fail, and the strongest of the other sexual components continues its activity as a perversion.[20]

REPRESSION. Another issue results if in the course of development certain powerful components experience a *repression*—which we must carefully note is not a suspension. The excitations in question are produced as usual but are prevented from attaining their aim by psychic hindrances, and are driven off into many other paths until they express themselves in a symptom. The result can be an almost normal sexual life—usually a limited one—but supplemented by psychoneurotic disease. It is these cases that become so familiar to us through the psychoanalytic investigation of neurotics. The sexual life of such persons begins [114] like that of perverts, a considerable part of their childhood is filled up with perverse sexual activity which occasionally extends far beyond the period of maturity, but owing to inner reasons a repressive change then results—usually before puberty, but now and then even much later—and from this point on without any extinction of the old feelings there appears a neurosis instead of a perversion. One may recall here the saying, "Junge Hure, alte Betschwester" (Young whore, old saint)—only here youth has turned out to be much too short. The relieving of the perversions by the neurosis in the life of the same person, as well as the above-mentioned distribution of perversion and

[20] Here one often sees that at first a normal sexual stream begins at the age of puberty, but owing to its inner weakness it breaks down at the first outer hindrance and then changes through regression to perverse fixation.

hysteria in different persons of the same family, must be placed side by side with the fact that the neurosis is the negative of the perversion.

SUBLIMATION. The third issue in normal constitutional dispositions is made possible by the process of "sublimation," through which the powerful excitations from individual sources of sexuality are discharged and utilized in other spheres, so that a considerable increase of psychic capacity results from an in itself dangerous predisposition. This forms one of the sources of artistic activity; and, according as such sublimation is complete or incomplete, the analysis of the character of highly gifted, especially of artistically disposed persons, will show any proportionate blending between productive ability, perversion, and neurosis. A subspecies of sublimation is the suppression through *reaction-formation,* which, as we have found, begins even in the latency period of infancy, only to continue throughout life in favorable cases. What we call the *character* of a person is built up to a great extent from the material of sexual excitations; it is composed of impulses fixed since infancy and won through sublimation, and of such constructions as are destined to suppress effectually those perverse feelings which are recognized as useless.[21] [115] The general perverse sexual disposition of childhood can therefore be esteemed as a source of a number of our virtues, insofar as it incites their creation through the formation of reactions.[22]

ACCIDENTAL EXPERIENCES. All other influences lose in significance when compared with the sexual discharges, shifts of repressions, and sublimations; the inner determinations for the last two processes are totally unknown to us. He who includes repressions and sublimations among constitutional predisposi-

[21] Certain character traits are known to stand in relationship to definite erogenous components. Thus obstinacy, stinginess, and orderliness are traceable to anal erotism. Ambition is determined through a marked urethral disposition.

[22] That keen observer of human nature, E. Zola, describes a girl, in his book *La joie de vivre,* who in cheerful self-renunciation offers all she has in possession or expectation, her fortune and her life's hopes to those she loves without thought of return. The childhood of this girl was dominated by an insatiable desire for love which whenever she was depreciated caused her to merge into a fit of cruelty.

tions, and considers them as the living manifestations of the same, has surely the right to maintain that the final structure of the sexual life is above all the results of the congenital constitution. No intelligent person, however, will dispute that in such a cooperation of factors there is also room for the modifying influences of occasional factors derived from experience in childhood and later on. It is not easy to estimate the effectiveness of the constitutional and of the occasional factors in their relation to each other. Theory is always inclined to overestimate the first, while therapeutic practice renders prominent the significance of the latter. By no means should it be forgotten that between the two there exists a relation of cooperation and not of exclusion. The constitutional factor must wait for experiences which bring it to the surface, while the occasional needs the support of the constitutional factor in order to become effective. For the majority of cases one can imagine a so-called "etiological group" in which [116] the declining intensities of one factor become balanced by the rise in the others, but there is no reason to deny the existence of extremes at the ends of the group.

It would be still more in harmony with psychoanalytic investigation if the experiences of early childhood would get a place of preference among the occasional factors. The one etiological group then becomes split up into two which may be designated as the dispositional and the definitive groups. Constitution and occasional infantile experiences are just as cooperative in the first as disposition and later traumatic experiences in the second group. All the factors which injure the sexual development show their effect in that they produce a *regression*, or a return to a former phase of development.

We may now continue with our task of enumerating the factors which have become known to us as influential for the sexual development, whether they be active forces or merely manifestations of the same.

PREMATURITY. Such a factor is the spontaneous sexual *prematurity* which can be definitely demonstrated at least in the etiology of the neuroses, though in itself it is as little adequate for causation as the other factors. It manifests itself in a breaking through, shortening, or suspending of the infantile latency period and becomes a cause of disturbances inasmuch as it provokes sexual manifestations which, either on account of the unready state of the sexual inhibitions or because of the undeveloped state of the genital system, can only carry along the character of perversions. These tendencies to perversion may either remain as such, or after the repression sets in they may become motive powers for neurotic symptoms; at all events, the sexual prematurity renders difficult the desirable later control of the sexual impulse by the higher psychic influences, and enhances the compulsive-like character which, even without this prematurity, would be claimed by the psychic representatives of the [117] impulse. Sexual prematurity often runs parallel with premature intellectual development; it is found as such in the infantile history of the most distinguished and most productive individuals, and in such connection it does not seem to act as pathogenically as when appearing isolated.

TEMPORAL FACTORS. Just like prematurity, other factors, which under the designation of *temporal* can be added to prematurity, also demand consideration. It seems to be established phylogenetically in what sequence the individual impulsive feelings are activated, and how long they can manifest themselves before they succumb to the influence of a newly appearing active impulse or to a typical repression. But variations seem to occur, both in this temporal succession as well as in the duration of the same, and these must exercise a conditioning influence on the end result. It cannot be a matter of indifference whether a certain stream appears earlier or later than its counterstream, for the effect of a repression cannot be made retrogressive; a deviation in time in the fitting together of the components regularly alters the result. On the other hand instinctive impulses appearing with special intensity often run a surprisingly swift course, as in the case of the heterosexual attachment of the later manifest homosexuals. The strivings of childhood which manifest themselves most impetuously do not justify the fear that they will lastingly dominate the character of the grown-up; one has as much right to expect that they will disappear in order to make room for their counterparts. (Harsh masters do not rule long.) To what one may attribute such temporal confusions of the processes of development we are hardly able to suggest. A view is opened here to a deeper phalanx of biological, and perhaps also historical, problems which we have not yet approached within fighting distance. [118]

ADHESION. The significance of all premature sexual manifestations is enhanced by a psychic factor of unknown origin which at present can be put down only as a psychological preliminary. I believe that it is the *heightened adhesion* or *fixedness* of these impressions of the sexual life which in later neurotics, as well as in perverts, must be added for the completion of the other facts; for the same premature sexual manifestations in other persons cannot impress themselves deeply enough to repeat themselves compulsively and to succeed in prescribing the way for the sexual impulse throughout later life. Perhaps a part of the explanation for this adhesion lies in another psychic factor which we cannot miss in the causation of the neuroses, namely, in the preponderance which in the psychic life falls to the share of memory traces as compared with recent impressions. This factor is apparently dependent on the intellectual development and grows with the growth of personal culture. In contrast to this the savage has been characterized as "the unfortunate child of the moment."[23] Owing to the oppositional relation existing between culture and the free development of sexuality, the results of which may be traced far into the formation of our life, the problem how the sexual life of the child evolves is of very little importance for the later life in the lower stages of culture and civilization, and of very great importance in the higher.

FIXATION. The influence of the psychic factors just mentioned favored the development of the accidentally experienced impulses of the infantile sexuality. The latter (especially in the form of seductions through other children or through adults) produce the material which, with the help of the former, may become fixed as a permanent disturbance. A considerable number of the deviations from the normal sex-

[23] It is possible that the heightened adhesion is only the result of a special intensive somatic sexual manifestation of former years.

ual life observed later have been thus established in neurotics and perverts from the beginning through the impressions received during the alleged sexually free period of childhood. The causation is produced by the responsiveness of the constitution, the prematurity, the quality of heightened adhesion, and the accidental excitement of the sexual impulse through outside influence.

The unsatisfactory conclusions which have resulted from this investigation of the disturbances of the sexual life is due to the fact that we as yet know too little concerning the biological processes in which the nature of sexuality consists to form from our isolated examinations a satisfactory theory for the explanation of either the normal or the pathological.